Ready made activities for
EFFECTIVE
COMMUNICATION
SKILLS

Ready made activities for EFFECTIVE COMMUNICATION SKILLS

Sheila Cane

the Institute
of Management
FOUNDATION
PITMAN
PUBLISHING

PITMAN PUBLISHING
128 Long Acre, London WC2E 9AN

A Division of Longman Group Limited

© Sheila Cane, 1994

First published in Great Britain 1994

British Library Cataloguing in Publication Data
A CIP catalogue record for this book can be obtained from the British Library.

ISBN 0 273 61177 1

10 9 8 7 6 5 4 3 2 1

Typeset by PanTek Arts, Maidstone, Kent.
Printed and bound in Great Britain by Clays Ltd, St Ives plc.

It is the Publishers' policy to use paper manufactured from sustainable forests

Contents

Foreword

I f there is one thing that most managers have in common, it is pressures on their time. In an increasingly hectic and competitive world, where change is the order of the day, there is rarely enough time for everything that needs to be done, and setting the right priorities is a prerequisite of success. Training can all too often take a back seat, even though it is a vital element in the pursuit of continuous improvement that is the hallmark of a successful company. It is acknowledged to be the archetypal 'good thing' yet, all too often, it ends up being neglected. So, anything that helps make training easier to implement and thus more certain to occur is all to the good.

This volume, in the *Ready Made Activities* series, is designed to do exactly this, providing a practical approach to developing the essential effective communication skills that are so crucial to the success of an organization in a competitive environment.

It is designed to set out guidelines to conducting a complete effective communication skills session, and is presented in the form of a training plan that is:

- *prescribed*, that is, the core content can be followed stage by stage, saving time in preparation, and ensuring that the coverage necessary to present the techniques and approaches fundamental to successful communication are presented thoroughly

- *participative*, giving clear information about how involvement can be included in a way that improves the learning prompted by the session

- *flexible*, arranged so that it can easily accommodate additional elements, particularly those designed to produce a focus on the individual communication requirements of the participants and organization involved

- *practical* and includes all the information necessary to run the session – with suggestions regarding examples, visuals, and the training techniques that are necessary to make it successful

all in a style that provides an appropriate and useful basis for **both line managers and those with little or no training or presentational experience to work from, as well as an aid to training specialists, perhaps especially those without a training background.**

After the Introduction, there is a section that sets out the way in which the material is presented and how it can be used. Thereafter, the material follows the sequence of the training session it describes, with support material afterwards for those who need additional guidance on the presentation of the material.

Having spent many years in a line manager role, I only wish I had had a series like this available, both for myself and to have helped me in developing the staff who worked for me in both our internal and external relationships. I am delighted to be part of this project, and by working from the point of view of what would have been useful for me, I hope that this volume will prove to be of value in raising the confidence with which your communicators perform.

Sheila Cane Training and Consultancy
67 Linton Street, London N1 7AN

Acknowledgements

First, I would like to express my thanks to Christina Saunders and Catalyst Human Resource Development Consultants with whom I have run many effective communication courses and with whom much of this workshop material was developed.

Second, I would like to thank Patrick Forsyth for being, as always, a valued provider of coffee, comments and support in the writing of this volume. Thanks are also due to Gower for giving permission to adapt some sections of Patrick's book, *Running an Effective Training Session* (Gower, 1992).

Third, I would like to thank David Sharp and all the staff at Pitman Publishing for their professional support and encouragement in the production of this series.

S.C.

1

. . . .

INTRODUCTION

Communication is the means by which we transfer ideas or information. To do so effectively means ensuring that our message is transferred clearly, without misunderstanding.

If it were easy, we would all be rich and successful and there would be no need for this book. However, it is the very reverse of easy. Organizations continue to spend more time and money on systems, organizational flow charts and the like to improve their efficiency and their relationships with customers, and yet all this effort may count for nothing unless the communication that results is clear and effective.

How an idea or information is communicated is often crucial to whether all the above is, or is not, translated into positive results for the organization.

Why is effective communication seen as being so difficult? Maybe because it doesn't always fit into a package of rules and techniques that ensure a successful outcome.

Does this mean that it is impossible to train staff to become better, more successful communicators? Certainly not.

Communication is an art. It is made up of techniques, a structure to provide support to the communicator, and well-developed interpersonal skills, as well as the instincts necessary to make the appropriate move at the right time. And, like all art forms, it can be learned by reviewing your actions, practice, and understanding what techniques increase the chances of a successful outcome.

Increasing the chances of effective communication

Communication must be undertaken in just the right way and its techniques deployed literally individual by individual, meeting by meeting, day by day. It involves all the interpersonal skills of demonstrating empathy, asking appropriate questions, and the ability to build relationships. It certainly isn't easy, as we all know to our cost. But it is possible to increase the likelihood of more successful communication by training.

If there is one factor that marks out a successful communicator, it is that they understand what makes them successful. This allows them to deploy techniques consciously, but always appropriately, to ensure that they have the desired effect. Experience can clearly help cultivate this ability, but it is not guaranteed to do so. Training can accelerate experience and can certainly develop the ability to review experiences so that lessons and even better techniques can be used. But training can never just happen – hence this book, the intention of which is to ensure that training in this area is made just a little easier and, thus, more likely to take place.

The approach taken in this book is a practical one, in part behaviour-driven, but also in part technique-driven. Above all, it is intended that anyone who has to communicate can go about their job with a heightened awareness that will allow them to use the appropriate techniques throughout their conversations. It is also intended to help them understand, and thus focus on, the other person's point of view, because only genuine two-way communication that shows respect and avoids being patronizing and pushy will lead to people wanting 'to do business' and create the sort of atmosphere where understanding and agreement thrive. This book is designed to help you to encourage your staff (whatever sort of role they have) to practise such an approach, and to set out clear guidelines to allow you to take them through the core skills and give them a foundation from which to work in future.

Who can best use this material?

Effective communication techniques do need to be applied differently depending on the situations and the individuals involved, but the skills and techniques themselves remain the same. Thus, this book has been prepared with a wide audience in mind.

The topic

The content relates to any face-to-face communication. It may be used in conjunction with other books in this series that focus on particular skills involving dealing with people.

The ideal participants

The content is designed to act as source material for a session directed at anyone whose job description involves dealing with people. Because much of the material will involve participants thinking about their own particular situations, we would suggest that groups should be made up of either individuals at a similar level in the organization or those who work together as a team.

The ideal 'leader'

The nature of the material makes it suitable for two broad groups of people.

- *Managers* in some sort of line or staff role that makes it logical for them to take responsibility for, and undertake, this sort of training. For these the material offers complete guidance, and flexibility, if required. It will save preparation time and make the conduct of a successful session more certain. It offers guidance on the running (that is, presentation and participative techniques) of a training session as well as structure and coverage.
- *Trainers*, who can either use it as a time saver (or to cross-check thinking with another source) for the more experienced, or to fill in gaps and build confidence for those less experienced.

Whichever category you fall into, the material is designed to be of practical help in improving the effectiveness of communication, and, thus, results.

HOW TO USE THIS MATERIAL

This material is designed to be self-explanatory and to minimize preparation time. Clearly you will need to read the material all the way through before embarking on running a training session, and you may also want to make additional notes to have with you to refer to during the session.

The material follows the sequence of the session it describes and is arranged so that its various elements stand out as signposts to the effective conduct of the session. Even the typeface has been chosen so that everything is presented in a size that may be read comfortably while standing in front of a group session.

As an overall plan of action, it is suggested that you:

- read this section first
- read through all of Sections 1 and 2
- check whether or not how you intend conducting the session will be aided by referring to the later material, which provides information about training techniques, and read through any elements you feel will be useful
- decide which elements of the programme you will use
- write out any notes you will need to have in front of you
- ensure that what you want to do relates to the nature of the group and the numbers who will attend, so that, for instance, participative elements will fit in
- check and arrange the equipment and environmental factors (a check-list to assist you with this process completes this section)

then you will be in a position to make final arrangements and conduct the session.

The main elements of the material

As you read on, you will notice that the material includes the following elements, which are commented on in turn.

Main content

The main thread of the material, in terms of suggested running instructions for the leader and detail of the coverage to be presented, appears sequentially. All main headings are in **large bold type** to facilitate rapid, easy reference as you conduct the session. All key instruction words, such as:

- **introduce**
- **explain**
- **discuss**
- **ask**

- **emphasize**
- **make a note**
- **stress**
- **summarize**

appear in **bold type** so that you know they are meant to be read as such.

In addition to this text, background notes give you more details about the topic under review. This design makes following the text easier on the day. Once you have read and digested this additional information, you may well wish to use it more as general background information than follow it slavishly, using the remaining, main text as the core material, enabling you to direct the session.

Symbols

Additional elements within the text are all flagged by appropriate symbols in the margin, again so that you can focus on all the different elements quickly and easily as you go through all the material. These include the following:

which stand for participation, visual and options.

Examples

There is a need in any training to exemplify points made in order to explain further and make them relate to the actual job done. Here, to do this, examples appear at various points in the text – as do spaces where you may wish to add examples relating to your own organization and, especially, to the products or services you supply. This provides a key opportunity to tailor the material more specifically to your own circumstances.

Visuals

Certain points are worth showing as well as saying (repetition and seeing as well as hearing are proven aids to learning). Suggestions as to which points to deal with in this way appear throughout the text. The simplest way in which to implement this is to write up material on a flipchart, or table top presenter. This can be done as the session progresses or made ready in advance and simply turned through as you go. Of course, if other methods are available, for instance an overhead projector, such material can be prepared as slides or written as you proceed using an acetate roll or sheets (see pages 132–3).

The suggestions take two forms in the text:

- a general suggestion is made to write something
- a specific suggestion is shown in the form that might result.

You can, of course, list more than is suggested and should look particularly for more visual images (within your artistic ability if you are using the flipchart or what is available that is already prepared).

Participation

Certain topics lend themselves to discussion or involvement, and, indeed, any meeting needs to include participation to maintain interest, improve learning, and make the link between the material covered and implementation. Clear suggestions appear at appropriate points, setting out participative elements that can be included – whether they are the simple asking of a question, brief discussion, or something more involved, such as an exercise or role playing. With an interactive skill such as communication, role playing is a proven way of improving awareness and bridging the gap between training and real-life situations. It is specifically suggested that each participant be given an opportunity to undertake a role play situation at each learning point. Basic details of how to set this up are given in context and more information about how to make role playing effective appears later (see page 146).

FLEXIBILITY OF THE MATERIAL

Whatever the configuration of your ideal training session, it may not be possible to proceed with exactly this as your structure. Some compromise is nearly always involved, especially regarding time and money. It is not always possible to spend as long on things, say, or include as much participation as you might wish. In addition, everyone's priorities vary, so that what is important in one organization may be less so in another, and taking more time over one element or topic may necessitate taking less over another.

The material is designed to be *flexible*. While it provides a comprehensive skeleton, the format allows additional tailoring towards the needs of a specific group – for instance, by adding examples, as mentioned earlier. To facilitate this process still further, certain elements of the programme may be regarded as *options* – that is, they may be omitted without disrupting the main thread of the content. This allows the material to be condensed somewhat, or for more tailoring (more added examples or participation, for example) to take place without extending the overall time the training takes.

At key points throughout the material, there is space for you to note timings. The precise timings will be conditioned by:

- the numbers attending
- the exact programme conducted
- the amount of planned and reactive participation
- the role play element

and, to some extent, the experience of the presenter.

Given manageable numbers (certainly six to ten) it should be possible to go through the suggested main content in one day. If necessary or desirable, you may want to schedule a longer or shorter session and you could even split the coverage in other ways (for example, by holding a series of evening sessions).

Make the material your own

Now, with these points in mind, you can proceed to the main training plan. It is *your* session we are talking about, so also remember one final point. As this book is designed to be a working tool, it is unlikely to do as good a job as is possible unless you overcome the natural reluctance most people have to write in a book. This book has been designed for you to write in it; no one will mind! So, do add your own notes and examples where appropriate and consider highlighting – in a second colour or with a fluorescent highlighting pen – to indicate the emphasis *you* want to make and to ensure that key points stand out. If you use the book to provide not simply guidance to conducting a session, but guidance to conducting *your* session, it will be that much more useful, and your participants will find what you put over that much more helpful to their work.

Further, if you aim to, or might, conduct workshops from this material more than once, then some additional note taking may well be useful. This results from the participative nature of any training. For example, if you make a point, then quote an example and ask for additional examples, you may well find that some good ones are volunteered. If so, some or all of these may be worth recording to use as part of the next presentation. In other words, your annotated material will become more valuable with use.

CHECK-LIST OF EQUIPMENT AND ENVIRONMENTAL FACTORS

This is a list of the kinds of things you will need to take into account and organize prior to a training session. It is not exhaustive so do add to it as necessary.

Equipment

Tables and chairs for you and delegates.

Glasses and water.

Pens and pads of paper.

Handouts (if used).

Flipchart stand, paper, and pens.

OHP, spare bulb, and acetate roll.

Video equipment (if used).

_____

_____

Things to check

That you know what the Fire Regulations are.

That you know where the toilets are.

That you know where coffee/tea will be.

That you know where lunch will be.

That enough refreshments will be available.

That the switchboard will stop calls to the phone in the room you will be using.

Who to ring if anything goes wrong.

That there is adequate ventilation.

That you minimize any noise (such as that from air conditioning).

_____

_____

Layout

Ensure that there is enough room for role plays and exercises.

Suggested layout

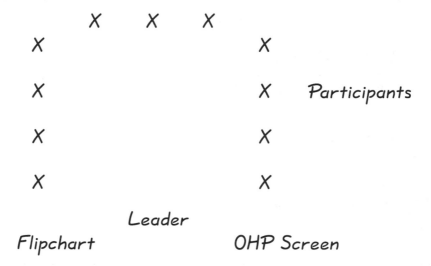

If you arrange the group in a horseshoe shape, you will ensure that they can see you as well as the flipchart and/or OHP. It also means that you will be able to see them.

If the room is not too narrow, the participants will also be able to pull their chairs back a little to make discussion spaces for small groups.

Before the role play sessions, you will be able to move most of the tables back against the wall and run the role play either in the middle of the room with the observers facing the action or in small groups well away from each other.

If the course is running for a day or longer, you may want to consider asking delegates to change places after the lunch break. It helps concentration to ring the changes occasionally (and also splits up cliques).

2

THE TRAINING SESSIONS

In this, the main part of the book, the plan for an effective communication workshop is laid out section by section. Having read the explanatory notes in Section I you will recognize the various elements as they appear, and will find that the guidelines on *how* to proceed through the sessions alternate with the *content* that needs to be conveyed to the participants.

Once you have been through this section, and personalized it to whatever degree you feel is useful (a process that can involve skipping elements as well as adding), then you should be able to conduct the session with these pages, and any visuals you decide to prepare, in front of you acting as your 'lecture/running order notes'.

Programme objectives

These are as follows:

- to *review* the essential techniques that make communication effective
- to *promote* a proven, flexible, and professional approach that makes practical sense in the real world
- to *develop* an understanding of how this approach can be used in both difficult situations and with challenging individuals
- to *prompt* a considered deployment of effective communication techniques as appropriate to each individual situation
- to *practise* all the elements in a safe environment
- to *build confidence* in implementing what has been learned.

Programme structure

Before going into the detail of the session, it may well be useful to get the overall shape of it in mind. The flow chart that follows sets out the various stages and elements graphically and is designed to enable you to keep the

COURSE MAP

Leader's notes

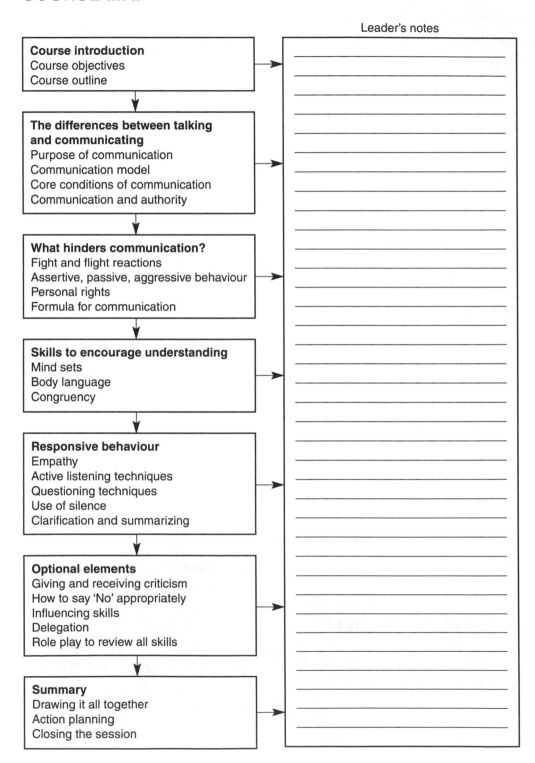

Course introduction
Course objectives
Course outline

The differences between talking and communicating
Purpose of communication
Communication model
Core conditions of communication
Communication and authority

What hinders communication?
Fight and flight reactions
Assertive, passive, aggressive behaviour
Personal rights
Formula for communication

Skills to encourage understanding
Mind sets
Body language
Congruency

Responsive behaviour
Empathy
Active listening techniques
Questioning techniques
Use of silence
Clarification and summarizing

Optional elements
Giving and receiving criticism
How to say 'No' appropriately
Influencing skills
Delegation
Role play to review all skills

Summary
Drawing it all together
Action planning
Closing the session

entirety of the session in mind throughout the process, so that individual elements are clearly put in context (this might usefully form the basis of a visual for use with the group as the session progresses).

The ruled spaces to the right of the diagram are designed for you to create your own individual running order including your own examples and exercises as appropriate to the group and the organization.

Session 1

···

Course introduction

Introduce yourself and ask the participants to introduce themselves, if they do not already know each other.

Explain any topical factors – internal or external – that make the course important *now*, for example:

● increased costs – need for higher productivity

● new ways of working – need for effective communication

● new teams/groups – need to build relationships

● after change – need for good communication/relationships

● competitive environment – need for more efficiency

● new initiatives – need to communicate effectively.

Make a note of any topical factors you will want to mention.

_____

_____

_____

_____

_____

Stress that none of the participants would be employed in their current positions if they were not effective communicators, but that everyone has some situations and individuals that they find difficult and this course is about helping make them easier and, thus, more effective.

Explain the objectives of the course (below), plus any others that you may wish to add.

 List these on the flip chart (or even leave them visible at the front throughout the session):

- *to review the essential techniques*
- *to promote a professional approach*
- *to develop understanding*
- *to prompt considered deployment*
- *to practise the processes*
- *to build confidence.*

Emphasize the practical nature of the programme.

 Ice breaker exercise. To draw attention to the complexities of communication, ask for or nominate a volunteer (A) to take your seat at the top of the table. Place a postcard of a black and white abstract design (a reproduction of a Mondrian painting is excellent) in A's hands (they must hold it up, quite still, in both hands at all times). Issue the participants with a black felt tip pen and plain white postcard each. The exercise is to ask A to describe in words *only* exactly what is on their card so that the participants make as perfect copies on their own cards as possible. The participants must not look at each other's cards but purely concentrate on what is being said to them and transcribe it.

The difficulty of this exercise lies in explaining size and positioning without any visual aids. The simpler the pattern, the shorter the time the exercise will take. Avoid any very complicated patterns and figures or letters. Instead use the kind of pattern shown on the following page.

Display the results and **ask** for comments before proceeding.

Explain the workshop coverage and link to the timetable (and any necessary administrative details – breaks, meals, where the toilets are, etc.).

 Prepared in advance:

Session 1:   Introduction

Session 2:   The differences between
              talking and communicating

Session 3:   What hinders communication

Session 4:   Skills to encourage understanding

Session 5:   Responsive behaviour

Session 6:   Specific situations

Session 7:   Summary.

Explain that, because the workshop is dealing with communication, it is likely that situations involving individuals some people find difficult will arise. Because of this, you want to discuss the issue of confidentiality.

Suggest that no individuals outside this group are named but rather that they are given pseudonyms and that the group do not discuss them outside the workshop. Second, **suggest** that it is fine for individuals to discuss what *they* said and did in this workshop, if they want to, but that it is *not* fine to discuss what any other individual did or said. **Ask** for comments and for agreement. **Stress** that everyone is free to raise this topic again at any time if they feel unsure about the confidentiality of the group.

Ask the group individually to list (by initials) everyone at work that they communicate with (at least 20, including colleagues, those in other departments, and customers) and mark them with a tick or a cross to indicate whether they find them easy or difficult to communicate with. Ask them to keep these lists for future reference.

Ask the group, using this list as a prompt, to consider what general aspects of communication they would specifically like to review in this workshop. Give them five minutes to do this on their own before asking them to share with a partner and add to their own objectives.

Ask them to read out their personal objectives in a plenary session.

List their objectives. **Add** specifics into Session 6, prompting if necessary whether anyone would like help with criticism, saying 'No', and influencing skills, including delegation.

Ask for any questions and comments before proceeding.

_____

_____

_____

_____

TIME:

BACKGROUND NOTES

Communication is the process by which information or ideas are transferred. To do so effectively means that the above is achieved clearly, without misunderstandings.

All of us are required to communicate all the time. Very little can be achieved in our lives without having to communicate, at work, at home, and with our friends. Most of the time we take our ability to perform the process effectively for granted and are genuinely surprised when a miscommunication happens.

Communication is the thread by which we, as individuals, are connected (or not) to the groups in which we operate. The stronger and more effective these threads are, the more contribution we will be able to make and the more our group will be able to achieve. This workshop has been designed to review the strengths of these threads and provide the skills and techniques to be able to strengthen any that show weaknesses.

Each of the participants will be an effective communicator most of the time or they would not be employed in the positions that they hold, but, none the less, all of us face some situations or individuals during our everyday lives that we find more difficult to communicate with than others. This programme is designed to make these occasions easier and, therefore, more likely to produce effective communication.

When communication is not effective, individuals, organizations, and society pay a very high price. We can all think of personal and working relationships that have been irretrievably damaged through misunderstandings. On a larger scale, nearly all the recent inquiries into major disasters (the Kings Cross fire, the Pan Am 103 explosion at Lockerbie, the deaths of vulnerable individuals in society, etc.) have concluded that a lack of effective communication was a major contributory factor.

The purpose of this programme is to consider in some detail what the purpose of communication is, how it differs from talking, how it is essentially a two-way process, and how it does not fit into a rigid set of rules. Because it is essentially dynamic, constantly changing according to the situation, we will review all the techniques that are of value and practise how to utilize them appropriately.

The benefits of increased effectiveness in communication for the individual can be seen in:

- increased confidence in difficult situations
- better relationships
- better understanding by and for others
- higher motivation for self and others
- better results and achievements
- increased promotion opportunities
- increased self-esteem.

The organization will benefit in terms of:

- better results and achievement of goals
- more effective use of resources (including time)
- reduced staff turnover and absence
- improved customer relationships
- more involvement of staff in better decision making
- increased development of workforce.

Any improvements that can be made in the effectiveness with which we communicate will pay enormous dividends to both the individuals concerned and the organizations within which we operate.

Session 2

The differences between talking and communicating

Explain that, for the purpose of this workshop, you will be considering all aspects of one-to-one, face-to-face communication, which, to create a visual image, we will refer to as a sender and a receiver.

 Draw the following visual image to refer to:

 Ask the group what the differences are between speaking and communicating and what might have happened if communication has been effective.

 List their answers, which might include:

- two-way process
- talking and listening
- feels good
- _____
- _____

Explain that talking may be one side of a communication but that it is essentially a two-way process that has to take the receiver into account if the message is to be received clearly.

Show (pre-prepared).

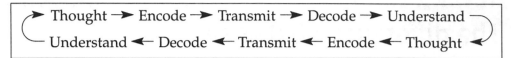

Thought → Encode → Transmit → Decode → Understand
Understand ← Decode ← Transmit ← Encode ← Thought

Explain the process (see further on page 30).

Stress that difficulties most usually occur in the encoding and decoding of the message.

 Ask for questions and comments.

 List the core conditions of communication:

- equality and respect
- empathy
- congruence.

 Ask the group for their thoughts on how a position of equality and respect enables effective communication and discuss.

 Show how the sender and receiver image is transformed by speaking up or down:

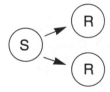

Stress that this destroys communication.

 Ask the group for a definition of empathy. Unless they are way off the mark, agree with everything they say, and ask if they can add anything.

Show them the workshop definition:

> Empathy is the ability to put yourself in someone else's shoes, to see and feel the world as they do without making a judgement as to whether they are right or wrong to see it or feel it as they do.

 Ask them for their thoughts on how empathy helps enable effective communication and discuss the points raised.

Explain that congruency exists when the words that we speak match the tone of voice and the body language that we use when we send our message.

 Ask them for their thoughts on how congruency helps (and incongruency limits) effective communication. Ask for volunteers to model both forms of behaviour.

 List the results. Effective communication demonstrates:

- respect to create equality
- empathy to develop understanding
- congruence to send a clear message.

 Ask for questions and comments before proceeding.

Explain that all the above lead to a win:win outcome in communication.

 Show

	win:win	
win:lose		lose:win
	lose:lose	

Discuss the results of each of the outcomes above (see further on page 33). **Stress** that win:win is the only outcome in an effective communication. **Ask** for questions and comments before proceeding.

Explain that, in the workplace, one of the most common areas of misunderstanding occur when the form of communication used is not clear.

 Show the following list (see further on page 34).

- *Request* – which the receiver has the right to refuse.
- *Instruction* – which may result in censure if refused.
- *Information* – which the receiver has the right to take or not.
- *Advice* – which the receiver has the right to take or not.
- *Prescription* – which may result in unwanted consequences if it is not taken.

Explain how the authority of both sender and receiver is seen on both sides and how this has a major impact on the extent to which these forms of communication are understood.

 Ask the group to go back to their notes of all the people they communicate with on a daily basis and consider whether there are any misunderstandings in terms of the above.

 Ask the group to split into two groups – one to discuss 'request' and 'instruction', and the other to discuss 'information', 'advice' and 'prescription'. Each group should choose a real-life situation and consider how it could be resolved.

 Ask each group to report back and discuss.

👉 **Ask** for any questions and comments.

👉 **Ask** them to share anything they have learned from this particular session.

✏️ **List** the contributions.

_____

_____

_____

_____

_____

_____

TIME:

BACKGROUND NOTES

Having said that communication is a skill that we take for granted when it is working effectively and are surprised when it breaks down, it is worth considering the differences between *talking* and *communicating*.

The purpose of *talking* is to say whatever it is that we want to without any particular attention being given to whether the message is received or understood correctly. So, we are likely to open our mouths and speak without thinking, sending words and messages without considering what impact they might have on the receiver.

The purpose of *communication* is to build a genuine understanding, a meeting of minds, so a communicator engages their brain before opening their mouth and considers what words, phrases or way of sending them might be likely to impart the thought in a way that helps it be received correctly.

In order to judge the effectiveness of a communication, it is necessary to judge the results. When we have been spoken to, we may understand what the sender meant, we may indeed even feel that we know what they want, but very rarely do we feel satisfied that it has been a two-way process in which we have made a contribution.

A working model of effective communication, then, might look like this:

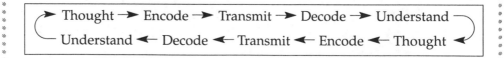

So, I have a thought, I put it into the sorts of words and phrases to send it in a way I think you will understand, and I send it to you. You listen to my message and decode it into your language and then decide whether you understand it (and indeed whether you agree or not). And then you repeat the process. Most of the time this process works fairly well.

Breakdowns in communication are most likely to happen in the area of encoding and decoding. If I know and understand you well, I am more likely to find the right words, phrases, and ways to transmit my message clearly, and because you know and understand me, you are more likely to decode them in the way I intend you to.

Carl Rogers, a distinguished psychotherapist, has laid down a series of what he calls the core conditions of counselling, which also work very well as conditions under which communication is likely to be effective. They are:

- equality and respect for the individual
- empathy
- congruency.

We are more likely to be able to communicate effectively if we have a genuine *respect* for the receiver and if we are able to create a position of *equality* with them. This means that when we meet someone we do not feel equal to or are in a situation in which we feel uncomfortable, we are likely to talk up or down to the receiver, which means that we are very unlikely to be able to communicate effectively. For example, if you meet the Prime Minister and are not able to put the role on one side, you will probably find yourself talking up to this person and no real communication will take place.

If, however, you can acknowledge the role and speak to the Prime Minister as an equal human being, then there *is* the possibility of communication. Similarly, for example, on public transport, if you have mislaid your ticket and want help, if you talk down to the ticket collector, you will be unlikely to achieve communication. However, if you can acknowledge the ticket collector's role and responsibilities and still ask for help from this person in a way that conveys that you see them as an equal human being, you will create the possibility of communication (*and*, incidentally, actually getting what you want).

A useful definition of *empathy* is that it is the ability to put yourselves in another's shoes, to see and feel the world as they do without making judgements as to whether they are right or wrong to feel the way they do. The more you think about this, the more difficult it is to achieve, but it is very important to try! It is linked with the previous condition of respect. It is only when we respect another person that we can respect their views and values. It is the opposite of the following kind of situation: we admit that we are afraid of a particular task, and someone else says, 'Oh, you shouldn't be afraid . . .'. This is a put down, making a judgement that someone should or shouldn't see or feel the world the way they do, and it guarantees that communication will break down. Empathy also gives insight into the words and phrases that they are more likely to under-stand in the same way that you do.

The third condition, *congruency*, is a concept that may be new to you. Often, this word is used in its negative form. We are all familiar with the concept of *in*congruency, where something is obviously out of line with the whole. *Congruency* in communication, therefore, means that every-thing I say matches my tone of voice and my body language. Lack of congruence exists when a child shouts 'I am *not* angry', when it is plain that their words are not the whole truth, that there is a part of the mes-sage that is not being communicated and, therefore, it is simply talking that is taking place. When our communication is congruent, the message comes across as being true and genuine.

When communication is effective it can be seen as sender and receiver demonstrating:

- respect to create equality
- empathy to develop understanding
- congruence to send a clear message.

It is important to realize that most of the time we do indeed perform very successfully and communicate effectively, but this workshop is about the occasions when it does not succeed. We will consider all the above conditions for communication in more detail later in the programme.

We will consider the occasions where, because we are uncomfortable with the particular situation or the individual concerned, breakdowns occur, as well as the times when we do not clarify sufficiently well to ensure that the message we have transmitted is the same as the one received. If you and I do not know each other well, or if either of us is uncomfortable with the other or the situation we are in, we are much more likely to encode and decode in a way that transforms the message into something that is completely different from what was originally intended.

One reason that communication breaks down can be demonstrated in the paradigm:

- win:win

- win:lose   - lose:win

- lose:lose.

Lose:lose is the situation in which both sides are so desperate to avoid conflict that they each agree to actions that are unacceptable to them. This agreement is very unlikely to last much longer than it takes to implement and, therefore, it might have been much better to have asked for time to consider what they really wanted.

Lose:win and win:lose have similar outcomes to the lose:lose situation. If I feel manipulated after a conversation during which I have agreed something because of pressure to do so or that you have got a better deal than I have, human nature being what it is, I am likely to be so upset that I will immediately plan how to take my revenge. Working with many groups of people over a period of some years, I am constantly amazed at how long we, as human beings, can hold these grudges. Sometimes it can take years to take revenge, but we usually get people back for feeling that we have lost out. Very often, if I have agreed to do something that afterwards I feel was unfair, I won't do it very well, so even the 'winner' in the conversation will end up losing.

Win:win is the only long-term successful outcome and it will result from effective communication. It means that both sides get something that they want, but without it being *at the cost* of the other. Each side feels that the result is fair and equitable and that they can walk away satisfied. As well as obtaining an agreement that is likely to work successfully, both parties, because they are satisfied with the result, have created a good working relationship and are likely to react positively to each other in the future. Rather than a game where one side wins and the other loses, effective communication is perhaps closer to a dance: both sides are in partnership with each other, and although one may lead and the other follow, there is a commitment to making each other look good.

Another area of communication breakdown that we can see often at work is the way in which authority and communication interrelate. In order to communicate, we phrase messages in many ways, some of which are:

- *request* – the receiver has the option of meeting it or not
- *instruction* – it is mandatory, so if it is not done, some sanction may be imposed on the receiver
- *information* – may be offered or sought, but what the receiver does with it is up to them
- *advice* – it may be offered or sought, but what the receiver does with it is up to them

- *prescription* – an authoritarian opinion from an expert/specialist; if the receiver does not follow it, some unwanted consequences may follow.

Often, in a working environment, there is a conflict between *instructions* and *requests*. A manager may ask a secretary to type a letter in the form of a *request*, but, if the secretary understands the manager's authority over the secretarial role, the secretary will *hear* it as an *instruction* and type the letter, to the satisfaction of both sides. If, however, someone the secretary considers to have no formal authority, makes the same request, the secretary may refuse and the other person may become angry. We tend to make requests because we want to be 'nice' when, really, we mean to convey instructions. It is important to clarify what authority the receiver understands us to have over them and to issue requests and/or instructions appropriately.

There is a similar confusion between *information*, *advice*, and *prescription*. If I am an expert or specialist (for example, a lawyer, an accountant, or tax specialist) my information or advice may take on the authority of a prescription, but only if you consider my authority, based on my qualifications, to be the same as I do.

When you are issuing an *opinion* as a *prescription*, it is important to clarify this – 'My legal opinion, is that you should . . .', as opposed to, 'I think you should . . .', which might just be a personal opinion. The implication in refusing to take prescriptive advice is that you will suffer the consequences that I laid out to you.

Often, in the workplace, we offer *advice* and *information* in the form of prescriptions. If you are not speaking with specialist authority, it is more effective to say so – 'I am not qualified in this area, but I think . . .'.

To avoid confusion, it is worth considering that *information* is offering facts without offering suggestions, an *opinion* is offering a personal view (without expertise), and a *prescription* is a qualified, expert view that is validated in some way.

The clarity with which the sender makes a communication and the way the receiver receives it depends on:

- how each perceives their own authority
- how each perceives the authority of the other.

If both sender and receiver have identical perceptions of each other's authority:

- the form of communication will be clear to them
- their role relationship will be clear to them.

Session 3

· ·

What hinders communication?

Explain that this session will consider what factors most commonly stop us communicating effectively and then introduce some strategies to handle them.

Explain the fight or flight syndrome (see page 41), which reduces effective communication, and introduce the terms *passive*, *aggressive*, *manipulative*, and *passive/aggressive behaviour*.

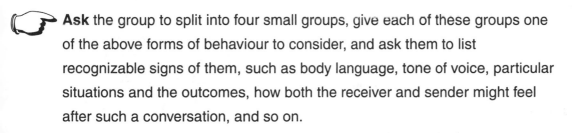 **Ask** the group to split into four small groups, give each of these groups one of the above forms of behaviour to consider, and ask them to list recognizable signs of them, such as body language, tone of voice, particular situations and the outcomes, how both the receiver and sender might feel after such a conversation, and so on.

Ask each group to report back and **discuss.**

Ask each participant to draw a line with 'passive' at one end and 'aggressive' at the other. **Explain** that, although we may react differently with different people, each of us will have an overall preferred form of reaction when threatened. **Ask** the participants to consider theirs and make a mark on the line to indicate where they think they tend to operate from when they are in a difficult situation.

Stress that when we are feeling comfortable, we are all assertive.

Ask the group for signs of assertive behaviour and **list** them, such as:

- good eye contact

- clear voice

- win:win outcome

- _____

- _____

Ask for questions and comments.

Explain that one of the most important ways of remaining assertive in a difficult situation is to give ourselves and those we are communicating with the following personal rights (**stress** that they are *two-way* rights).

- be treated with respect
- have and express feelings and opinions
- be listened to and taken seriously
- set our own priorities
- say 'no' without feeling guilty or selfish
- ask for what we want
- ask for information from others
- make mistakes and be wrong
- choose *not* to assert ourselves
- consider our needs as important as the needs of others.

Read them through out loud. Explain that there is probably at least one that is difficult even to consider taking on board.

Ask the group to consider these rights carefully and discuss.

Explain that, when you are in a difficult situation, taking on and giving these personal rights will help you remain assertive, but you will still need a structure to communicate effectively. Such a structure consists of the following:

- set the objective and a fall-back position
- plan strategy
- state purpose and reason
- encourage the receiver to respond
- negotiate
- agree action
- clarify
- check how each of you are feeling.

Explain each step.

 Ask for questions and comments.

Explain that it is valuable to practise and rehearse difficult situations in a safe environment before trying out new strategies. Explain that you are going to ask them to role play simple prescribed situations using all the above. Ask for any concerns about role play and resolve them if possible.

 Show the following role play ideas:

- ask your manager for information that he or she doesn't want to give you
- ask a colleague to cover for you (you have a social engagement)
- ask a subordinate to do a menial task (one that is not part of their job).

Explain that you want them to work in groups of three, taking turns to be the sender, receiver, and observer, for ten minutes each. The purpose is to practise the structures rather than to 'win' the conversation. The sender should choose the situation that is most difficult for them, and try to be assertive and achieve effective communication. The receiver should not try to be assertive and should react as the sender makes them want to. The observer should make notes as to what they observed helped the communication. (See page 148 for guidelines for workshop leaders.) It does not matter if they each choose the same situation as they can learn from each other.

☞ **Role play**.

☞ **Discuss** the results together in a plenary session.

☞ **Summarize** this section.

☞ **Ask** for things learned during the session and **list** them.

_____

_____

_____

_____

☞ **Ask** for questions and comments and note the best ones.

_____

_____

_____

_____

TIME:

BACKGROUND NOTES

Effective communication is based on respect and equality, showing empathy, and speaking with congruency, and may be recognized in the following behaviour (assertive):

- relaxed body language, mirroring the other
- comfortable eye contact
- space for both to speak
- each sentence builds on the previous one
- both sides feel comfortable at the end.

What happens to stop us communicating in those situations where it is important for us to do so but we are feeling uncomfortable? To find the answer, we need to go back in time.

When our ancient forebears were going about their daily tasks and a sabre-toothed tiger appeared from behind a rock, the physiology of these people immediately reacted to the threat by producing all the physical reactions necessary to enable them to either fight and kill the tiger or to run away and hide – called the *fight or flight syndrome*. Unfortunately, our physiology has not evolved fast enough to keep up with the changes that have happened since, so now, when the Managing Director asks us a tricky question, our bodies react in exactly the same way. But it is *not* appropriate to run as far away as possible or to beat up the Managing Director even though this is exactly what we *want* to do. So, we exhibit forms of behaviour that mirror the fight or flight syndrome.

Aggressive behaviour stems from the *fight* reaction. We can recognize it in some or all of the following behaviours:

- raised, loud, clipped voice
- clenched fists, banging table, waving arms
- staring, invasive eye contact
- intimidating body language, moving closer, standing up
- flushed face
- not listening, no space to respond.

The *flight* reaction may be seen in *passive* behaviour, which can take some or all of the following forms:

- withdrawn eye contact, looking down, hiding behind hair
- withdrawn body language, hiding, looking smaller
- words, including 'sorry' and continual agreement
- as little verbal response as possible
- pale or blushing skin
- face angled downwards.

There are also less obvious ways of exhibiting these forms of behaviour. Someone who by nature is aggressive when threatened, but who is trying to hide this, may take on what is known as *manipulative* behaviour. Because this is a covert behaviour, it is often difficult to recognize any signals of it, but the results will always leave the receiver feeling uncomfortable. For example, if the receiver asks if it would be all right if they went out with their friends for the evening and the sender says, 'Of course, it is. You go and have a good time. Don't worry about me, I'll just sit and watch television even though there isn't anything worth watching. You just go and have a good time.' Although the receiver will have been given permission in the words, it is clear that it isn't the way the sender feels, and so the receiver will almost certainly feel guilty and, most likely, *not* go and have a good time.

Similarly, someone who by nature is passive when threatened is unlikely to be able to declare what they would really like and will often exhibit *passive/aggressive behaviour*. For example, being late and taking sick leave is likely to indicate that the sender isn't happy at work, but is unable to say so or act assertively to improve things. Often people who are inclined to react passively are uncomfortable saying 'no' because they want to be liked and end up doing things unwillingly because they think it will give them the results they want. Unfortunately, this often has such unsatisfactory results that the relationship is damaged far more than if they had said 'no' when originally asked.

To sum up, the results may be seen as follows:

- *passive:*
  - certain of rejection
  - resigned to defeat
  - gives up all rights
  - avoids conflict
  - short-term success
  - long-term dissatisfaction
  - feels frustrated, unhappy
  - lose:win

- *aggressive:*
  - reject first in case others reject
  - attack the best form of defence
  - takes away receiver's rights
  - creates conflict
  - short-term success
  - long-term dissatisfaction
  - feels defensive, belligerent
  - win:lose.

We cannot banish all the 'sabre-toothed tigers' from our lives, so how do we manage our reactions to them? As many people have found, to acknowledge and hold the following *personal rights*, as well as giving them to those we wish to communicate with, is valuable to achieving such management.

- be treated with respect
- have and express feelings and opinions
- be listened to and taken seriously
- set our own priorities
- say 'no' without feeling guilty or selfish

- ask for what we want

- ask for information from others

- make mistakes and be wrong

- choose *not* to assert ourselves

- consider our needs as important as the needs of others.

Achieving some of these will be harder for us than others. Also, some of them we will have already given to the people we wish to communicate with and others will be more difficult.

The right to be treated with respect is the key to creating the equality that encourages communication. If we give ourselves the right to be treated with respect and give it to others, it will be impossible to talk up or down to another person.

The right to have and express feelings and opinions is the key to having the confidence necessary to make a contribution to any communication. By giving others this right, we encourage them to engage in two-way communication.

The right to be listened to and taken seriously links in with the previous right and encourages the opinions and contribution of others.

The right to set our own priorities is one that is often ignored at work. Every right carries with it a responsibility to own the consequences and this is particularly apt in this instance. For example, if I choose to live in our society but wish to have a lot of money without working for it, I may choose to rob a bank, in which case I may achieve my objective, but I may well also have to live with the consequences – serving a lengthy prison sentence. Similarly, at work, if I choose not to start work before midday, I may have to pay the consequences of losing my job. I might, however, be able to find a job where this action is acceptable. It is my choice to set my own priorities *so long as* I own the consequences of my actions.

The right to say 'no' without feeling guilty or selfish is based on the level of our self-esteem and is one many people find very difficult. It is often easier to give this right to others than to accept it ourselves. It involves a little effort, taking it on board, and, perhaps, trying it in low-risk situations before taking on sabre-toothed tigers!

The right to ask for what we want is also based on the health of our self-esteem and takes some effort to put into action. It also may involve giving some serious consideration to what it is exactly that we do want.

The right to ask for information links with the last right mentioned above. Often we are intimidated by 'experts' – doctors, lawyers, and so on – and deny ourselves this right. But taking it on may make a large difference to the contributions you allow yourselves to make in communications.

The right to make mistakes and be wrong is often one that causes difficulty. This right does not mean that we *intend* to make mistakes, but, rather, that *when* they happen (which our human nature ensures will surely happen), we will learn from them quickly and move on rather than beating ourselves up for making them. Most of our learning comes from making mistakes and learning from them, so we should welcome rather than dread mistakes. This is again a right we often find easier to give to others than accept for ourselves.

The right to choose *not* to assert oneself is a saving grace in a list of very positive statements. It means that we do not *always* have to be positive, dynamic, and assertive. We can choose to take the easy way out sometimes and feel OK about this. This is one that some people genuinely find harder to give to others than themselves.

The final one is often the most important. The right to consider our needs as important as the needs of others. *As*, that is, not *more*. Often we find ourselves putting others' needs first and then find that we haven't the stamina or resources to complete what we have agreed to do because we allowed our needs to be subservient to others'.

All these rights, when accepted as our own and given to others, will help manage threatening situations when they occur and stop us from reacting with passive or aggressive behaviour.

So, how do we put all this into operation when we are considering a communication? Remember the structure for effective communication:

- set the objective and a fall-back position
- plan strategy
- state purpose and reason
- encourage the receiver to respond
- negotiate
- agree action
- clarify
- check how each of you are feeling.

Before any communication, it is important to check *why* you are intending to communicate; what is the purpose of it? And, if there is not a *two-way* win:win purpose, then forget it. For example, if I want to make you look foolish or win your approval at all costs, then I can only talk, it will not be possible to communicate. However, if there is a two-way win:win purpose, such as improving our working relationship, then continue.

The next step is to clarify what your ideal outcome would be; this becomes your objective. Unless you are clear about your objectives, how will you know whether you are satisfied or not with the outcome? If you want a pay rise, decide how much you want, when you want it and so on. A good way of checking your objectives is to make them SMART:

- S = simple
- M = measurable
- A = achievable
- R = realistic
- T = timed.

So, if you want a pay rise of £1000 per annum, to be payable from the end of the month, and you believe that this is both realistic and achievable, then you have a SMART objective. If you just want a pay rise without any SMART conditions, then I might agree to give you one in five years' time. You would feel unhappy, but you would still have got what you asked for! This is why SMART objectives are so helpful – they add clarity, give you standards to measure against, and aid effective communication.

The next step is to remember that if this communication is to result in both of us achieving a win:win outcome, I may not get everything I want, so I need to think about what my fall-back position would be, what I could achieve and still walk away feeling satisfied (my bottom-line condition for satisfaction). Following the example of a pay rise, this might be that you understand that I think I deserve a pay rise and that you agree to consider it in six months' time. Also, I need to introduce what I think might be in it for you so as to create an atmosphere of two-way win:win. If I *can't* think what might be in it for you, I might have to ask you. If I have been doing an important task that will reflect well on you, it might be appropriate to remind you of this or simply that I will be happier and more comfortable doing this task if I am properly rewarded for doing it.

Having set your objectives and a fall-back position, the next step is to consider your strategy. Where will you have this meeting? In the corridor or in a private meeting room? What time of day would be best for both of you? How much time will you need to ask for? Will you need to prepare and bring papers with you? Consider how you will respond to what you expect their responses to be.

When you ask for the meeting, it is important to create the right impression. Ask for a meeting with specific time boundaries (then stick to them) and tell them what the subject of the meeting is. Too often, at work people ask for a minute when they mean at least 15 and then belittle their concerns – 'I have a little problem . . .', or, 'There is a bit of a problem . . .'.

Neither of these is likely to create the right atmosphere for what is a serious subject for you.

A strategy should never be set in stone. Consider it as you would a route map. For example, if you want to drive from one city to another, you may have a choice between a direct motorway route or a more interesting country route and plan to take one of these two routes. If there are roadworks on the route you've chosen, though, what do you do? You branch off as soon as possible and take another road until you have passed the obstruction. Is this a failure? Certainly not. It is achieving your goal in the most effective way possible. It is the same in communication: whatever your strategy, when you hit an impasse it makes sense to adjust your route until you can get back on course. Communication has all sorts of similarities to a dance and if your partner suddenly wants to spin and turn another way, it makes sense to go with them and slowly bring them back to the direction you want to go in. Two-way communication involves *at least* some consideration of what they want – give and take is the key.

When the meeting starts, state what you want using 'I' instead of 'we', 'you', or 'they'. Only by speaking from a personal standpoint can you convey that it is important to you. Also, it comes across much more powerfully than if you dilute the message by sharing it with unspecific others. If you are speaking on behalf of a group, though, make this clear. For example, 'I have been asked by the rest of the team to speak to you on their behalf.'

When you have stated your opening position, encourage them to respond. You might need to ask them a question about how they feel about what you have just said, then continue the conversation by acknowledging what they have said, and move towards a negotiated win:win outcome (remembering your fall-back position). For example:

' I feel I deserve a pay rise for . . . . What do you think?'

'I can't even consider any pay rises now.'

'I understand that it would be difficult for you to consider a pay rise now. Do you see, though, why I think I deserve one? Is it possible that you might be able to reconsider soon?'

Listen carefully to each of their responses so that you can make it clear that you have understood their position and move towards an agreement.

When you have an agreement, clarify it so that both of you are clear about the outcome. How often do we leave meetings thinking completely different things have been agreed? An example of such clarification could be as follows:

'Thank you for your understanding that I feel I deserve a pay rise. I appreciate that it is impossible for you now, but we have agreed to meet again at the end of November to discuss this again.'

If possible, check how they are feeling. It will only be a win:win outcome if both of you are feeling comfortable. For example:

'Thank you for this meeting. I feel better now that I have spoken to you about my salary. How do you feel about it?'

Obviously, different organizations and different relationships will require different words and phrases that will encourage understanding; the above examples are only guidelines to illustrate the process.

Session 4

Skills to encourage understanding

 Show

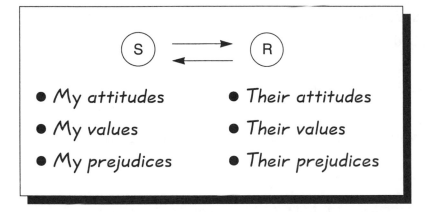

Explain that, in order to communicate effectively, it is important to understand the part mind sets play.

 Ask the members of the group to each take a sheet of paper and describe in words the sort of person, including their age, they imagine when they hear or see the following names: (choose alternatives, where appropriate, for the group or organization involved):

Tracey/Sharon	Mary
Darren/Elvis	Rupert/Crispin
Albert/Sidney	Octavia
Florence/May	George

Discuss the results.

Options This exercise may also be done with portraits cut from magazines or putting on flip chart paper the answers to questions such as, 'All managers/bosses/salespeople/men/women/secretaries/juniors are . . .'.

Discuss how mind sets limit effective communication. Not only about who we think the person is, but how we hear certain words and phrases that we also have prejudgements about.

Explain that we cannot avoid making judgements, but, when we are aware of them, we can put them on one side and look at the individual rather than our mind set about them.

 Ask for questions and comments.

Explain that congruency is also important to avoid sending mixed messages.

 Show the group the following statistics about how the impact of communication is divided up (see further on page 57).

• Visual	55 per cent
• Tone of voice	37 per cent
• Words	8 per cent.

Explain that this is why we don't take most notice of the words when a child shouts 'I am *not* angry.'

 Ask for other examples and discuss. Ask what sorts of things might lead to sending mixed messages and how we can avoid sending them.

Explain that body language and tone of voice will nearly always give away emotions that we are trying to hide. For example, when we are nervous, upset, angry or unsure of what we are saying, it is likely to be apparent to the receiver. The only way to send genuine messages clearly and congruently is to prepare as fully as possible and to tell the whole truth.

Explain that it is also important to understand how we come across to others. We may think we are sending one message when the people we are trying to communicate with are receiving another.

 Exercise. Ask each participant to write their name at the top of a copy of the Impression management list that follows and ring one word in each category that they think best describes them (they may ring two if they think both are applicable or add another word that they think better describes them).

This exercise requires silence and concentration to allow genuine feedback. Some groups find it difficult to do, but the results are always valuable.

Impression management

Name:

Eye contact	direct, evasive, hesitant, dominating
Posture	upright, vigorous, slouching, nervous
Facial expression	pleasant, grim, open, closed, smiling
Voice	clear, gruff, high-pitched, hesitant, soft
Attitude	friendly, dictatorial, condescending, passive
Manner	positive, shy, relaxed, dynamic
Appearance	smart, scruffy, clean, tidy, attractive

When everyone has finished, ask them to pass their list to the left.

Explain that, when a list comes to you, you have to add a small tick to the word in each category that you think best describes the way the person whose name is at the top comes across to you. Try not to be too influenced by what other people think. Keep passing the sheets round until everyone has added to each sheet, then pass them back to the person whose name is at the top. Allow people time to read them.

Ask if anyone has any surprising results. Explain that one tick on a word that doesn't fit their view of themselves probably isn't relevant, but two or more might provide a clue that they are not coming across as they think they are. Ask if anyone has several surprising ticks. Ask if they would like additional feedback, and, if so, ask the group to participate. For example, if James has four ticks on hesitant eye contact, will anyone admit to being one of the four and be prepared to tell him what specifically he does that led you to tick that word? Encourage people to 'own' their feedback, add your own if appropriate, saying, for example, 'James, would you like additional feedback from me? I notice that when you are unsure, you seem to drop your eyes away. Does that ring a bell for you?' Take each person in turn and allow them as much time as they need to check out their feedback, try to make sure that each person feels that they have dealt with their feedback completely before moving on to the next.

Discuss the results.

Summarize the session and ask for things learned and **list** them.

_____

_____

TIME:

BACKGROUND NOTES

Mind sets, prejudices, frames of reference, or prejudgements all get in the way of communication and need to be acknowledged before they can be set aside. Every time we look at someone, we automatically categorize them and thus limit their contribution to us. This is quite normal and everyone does it. We fit people into boxes, such as age, gender, class and background, colour of skin, colour of hair, style of clothes, their names, their jobs . . . the list is endless.

It is impossible to create a position of equality with someone we have put into a box of judgements and therefore to communicate effectively with them. It is also impossible *not* to make these judgements, so what do we do?

Once we are aware of the judgements we are making, it is easier to put them on one side. We need to become more aware of the mind sets that we have and then be prepared to put them on one side.

It is also important to be aware that the receiver in any communication will also have their own mind sets about *you* and the words that *you* use. The more you can use empathy, the more you will become aware of such judgements and then be able to help the other person put them on one side. For example, if I think you overreact whenever I use the word 'criticism', I might choose to ask you what it is you take it to mean when I say it and see whether we can resolve any differences in understanding, or simply to use a similar but hopefully less emotive word, such as 'feedback', to encourage you to hear what I need to say.

In order to communicate effectively, it is important to be aware of and take responsibility for how your message is received as well as how you send it. For example, it doesn't matter what I think of the word 'criticism' or what I mean by it, my only concern should be what is your reaction when I use it. If your reaction leads me to believe that you are receiving a different message than the one I am intending, then, if I am committed to us achieving effective communication, I must do something to resolve the potential breakdown.

If you feel the receiver has made a restrictive judgement about you that is getting in the way of you communicating effectively, it may be difficult to find an appropriate way of helping to clear it. The best thing to do may be not to refer to what you think the problem is, but to concentrate on the positive vision of what you would like your relationship to be like. If you can 'sell' them your commitment to having a great relationship, they will almost certainly revise their judgements. Think for yourself how often you have had to spend time with someone about whom you had a restrictive mind set and then revised it in light of your experience of them.

Another way of helping the receiver of your communications to receive your message clearly is to be congruent at all times. When we are feeling comfortable, we are able to speak what is the truth for us congruently and the message is received clearly. But, when we are feeling uncomfortable, we often send mixed messages – that is, when the tone of voice that we use and our body language is not appropriate for the words that we are saying. Shouting 'I am *not* angry' is a prime example of this. It is important to be aware that when we lie or even stretch the truth, our body language and the tone of our voice give us away. Congruency has sometimes been called 'the words and music' and when these match, as in a dramatic opera or a pop song, we can understand what the meaning is even if the words are in another language.

So, an effective communicator needs to be able to listen to the 'music' (the tone of voice and body language) to see if it matches the words and then, rather than make a snap judgement ('He's just been told off by the MD', or 'She's having a bad day'), check it out for ourselves.

Some examples of mixed message behaviour follow.

- When people are rude or aggressive, they may be trying to say that they are feeling threatened or unfairly treated.

- When people are slow and refuse to hurry, they may be trying to say that they are feeling hassled, pushed, and are asking you to leave them alone.

- When someone disagrees with you in public or puts you down, they may be getting their own back for something they perceived you did to them some time ago, of which you may be completely unaware.

- When people refuse to make decisions or will neither agree nor disagree with you, they may be implying that, because you are the manager, it is up to you to make the decisions.

- When people laugh or giggle, they may be trying to let you know that they are embarrassed or afraid or feel that it is too private to discuss.

Often we *deliberately* send a mixed message. For example, if we have made a fool of ourselves by, say, falling over in the corridor and someone asks how we are, we tend to say 'I am fine' with a very un-fine tone of voice and body language. This is because we *want* to be fine and hope you will think we are. However, it is not a very effective form of communication. It might be more assertive and genuine to say, 'Right now, I am feeling dreadful, but, in a moment or two, I am going to be fine. Thank you for asking.'

In research done for Kodak it was found that the information we receive breaks down as follows in terms of the impact of aspects of its presentation:

- visual   55 per cent
- tone of voice   37 per cent
- actual words   8 per cent.

So, although we may worry endlessly about the exact *words* to use, research tells us that only 8 per cent of our message will be received through that medium. Therefore, it is important to be aware of how we normally come across to other people. It is rare that we have an opportunity to hold a mirror up to our behaviour and begin to see ourselves as others do, but this is very important if we are to manage our communication more effectively. As the term 'body language' implies, our bodies send their own messages. If I think I come across as a pussy cat and six other people tell me that they see me as a gorilla, I might decide to adjust my body language to achieve the impression that I intend to make. One word of caution, though: before you do this, take as wide a sample as you can because one comment may say more about the other person than it says about you. For example, a timid person may well see someone who is slightly less timid than them as being confident and outgoing.

Many people have changed their body language and tone of voice in order to come across more effectively. Sometimes, just standing better and straighter will enable you to send your messages with more power and vitality. Also, it has been widely reported that Margaret Thatcher lowered her voice by several tones before she was elected Prime Minister.

There are very few rules about body language and it is dangerous to make too many assumptions. Folding of the arms may well mean that we are feeling threatened, but it may also simply mean that we are feeling cold! What one individual will see as open and relaxed eye contact may be intimidating to another. We need to be aware of how we are coming across to each individual by observing their reactions to us and responding appropriately. If I am talking to you and you are sitting right back in your chair and moving away from me, I might try to lessen the intensity of my message. If that does not seem to help, I might ask you whether or not you are comfortable.

In an effective communication, you will find that both parties will be performing a 'dance': their body language will begin to mirror each other's, they will move their chairs so that they are comfortable with the distance from each other, then, as they reach agreement, they will move closer to each other and are quite likely to touch to signal consensus – maybe this is the origin of the tradition of the handshake on completing a deal?

Being aware of how we come across to others is valuable in recognizing why sometimes we don't communicate effectively.

Being more aware of how others receive our visual messages gives us an opportunity to tailor our message more carefully in situations where success is important but where we are not particularly confident and comfortable.

Session 5

Responsive behaviour

 Show

Explain, in relation to the above, that, so far, we have been focusing on how the sender can put across their message more effectively, but that for this session we are going to concentrate on the other side of two-way communication – responding to a message so that we can receive and understand it effectively.

Remind the group of the workshop definition of empathy.

 Empathy is the ability to put yourself in someone else's shoes, to see and feel the world as they do without making a judgement as to whether they are right or wrong to see and feel it as they do.

Explain that it is the key to being able to respond effectively, because only when we can put any prejudgements on one side are we able to truly listen. And it is only when we are aware of what our prejudgements are that we can put them to one side.

Discuss and ask for questions and comments.

Explain that you are going to review good active listening skills.

Ask the group to form pairs and move their chairs so that they face each other and decide which of them will listen first (A) and second (B) as they do the following exercises.

Exercise 1

A and B both speak simultaneously for one minute on how they got to the workshop this morning.

Review what has happened. Ask what it was like to listen while speaking and speak when the other was speaking. List the conclusions arrived at.

 List these conclusions, which might include that you need to be quiet to listen.

Exercise 2

A takes up a rock-like position – no eye contact, no body movements, no sound. B speaks for two minutes on 'things that I enjoy about my job'.

Change roles and repeat.

Review what has happened. Ask for feedback. How was it for both speaker and listener? What is required to improve it?

 Add to the list made at the end of Exercise 1, such as: the listener needs to encourage the speaker, look interested.

Exercise 3

A listens, using as much eye contact and body movement as they want to and encouraging sounds (umm, aarh, mm mm, and so on), but no real words. B speaks for two minutes on 'things that I find difficult in my job'.

Change roles and repeat.

Review what has happened. Ask for feedback. How was it for both speaker and listener? What is still required for improvement?

 Add to the list made at the end of Exercise 1, such as that words and questions are important.

Exercise 4

Participants turn away from their partners with pencil and paper and answer the following questions.

● What colour are your partner's eyes?

● What colour and style is your partner's hair?

● What colour shirt/tie/jacket/other items are they wearing?

● Describe the accessories (say, glasses, watch, ring) they are wearing.

● Describe the shoes and socks/tights they are wearing.

The participants turn back to face each other and check whether or not their answers are correct.

Discuss the results and remind participants about the results of Kodak's research.

 Add to the list made at the end of Exercise 1, adding such points as that it is important to listen with the eyes.

Exercise 5

With their partners again, A describes a recent work project or holiday, giving as many technical facts and details as possible. B listens (without taking notes) taking in as much as they can absorb, then interrupts appropriately to summarize and check their received information. A continues, after these interruptions.

After five minutes, A and B change roles and repeat.

Discuss what happens.

 Add to the list begun at the end of Exercise 1, adding points like you need to summarize more often than you think.

Discuss all five exercises and ask for questions and comments.

Explain that we can summarize what has been learned in the letters of the word LISTEN (see further on page 67):

- L = look interested
- I = inquire with questions
- S = stay on target
- T = test understanding
- E = evaluate the message
- N = neutralize your feelings.

Explain and **discuss** each point.

A final exercise. Divide the group into pairs with new partners, and spread them about the room so that they have some space. Explain that each is to encourage their partner to speak about their latest achievement for ten minutes, using all the above skills and techniques. The listener is to manage the exercise – that is, it should not turn into a conversation, but the listener is to encourage the speaker to talk. Stress how difficult it is to stay on target and suggest questions like, 'So, what have you learned from this achievement that you can use elsewhere?', 'What was it that made it such an achievement?', and so on. Decide who is going to listen first. The listener starts by saying, 'Tell me about your latest achievement.'

(Note that the leader may need to facilitate each group for a while. Let the exercise run the full ten minutes, then each partner is to thank the other, change roles and chairs and repeat.)

Review the exercise by asking how it was to listen and how it was to be listened to with such attention.

Discuss the points raised.

Summarize how listening is taken for granted, how hard it is to do well, and how satisfying it can be for both sides when some care is taken in this area. Although there seems such a lot to do when listening, explain that we *talk* at approximately 120 words per minute, but that we can *listen* at 240 words per minute, so there *is* time to do it well. Also, remind the group that we each have *two* ears, but only *one* mouth, and, perhaps, this should remind us that we need to listen twice as much as we talk.

Ask for things the participants have learned from the session and **list** them.

_____

_____

_____

TIME:

BACKGROUND NOTES

This session stresses that effective communication is two-way, that it needs to involve the receiver, helping them understand the message correctly, as much as the sender thinking about how they code and send it.

Empathy is the key to understanding more about another individual. The more we can be aware that the world may be very different for others and, where appropriate, the more the sender can ask questions of the receiver to discover how *they* see and feel the world (or the subject under discussion) the better. In the relationships where we feel comfortable, this has probably already taken place and it is certainly true that we tend to make friends with people who have similar views to ourselves.

Empathy is the opposite of having preconceived views. It allows us the freedom to discover what the truth is for the sender, even if it is very different to our own. Using empathy is the first step in opening up possibilities in the situations in which we find it difficult to communicate effectively.

It is also very important to listen *actively*, rather than *passively*, as is more usual. Listening is, perhaps, a forgotten art in our fast-moving, modern world of supposedly increased communication and technologies. It is possible that we wouldn't have to work quite so hard at communicating if people would only listen a bit more actively. The first step in this transformation is to consider what active listening consists of.

A useful prompt is LISTEN, the letters standing for the essential elements of active listening, which, just to recap, are:

- L = look interested
- I = inquire with questions
- S = stay on target
- T = test understanding
- E – evaluate the message
- N = neutralize your feelings.

Looking interested means giving the sender of the communication your full attention. Turn your body towards the sender, give them as much direct eye contact as they seem comfortable with. Smile and look welcoming as regards their message. Show them that you are interested, making 'hmm' and 'ah' noises to encourage them to continue speaking.

Inquiring with questions involves asking open questions to encourage them to develop any point that you are not sure you understand. An *open question* is one to which it is not possible to answer with one word, and usually begins with 'who', 'what', 'where', 'how', or, occasionally, 'why', although you have to be careful with this last one as it may come across as challenging.

A *closed question* may give you the answer you want, but often it will not be the truth – 'Do you understand?' being a prime example of a closed question people answer 'yes' to even though they do *not* understand. It is a brave person who says 'no'. A more effective question might be, 'What have you understood?' or even, 'So, what do you think would be a good plan of action to achieve this?'

When listening, it is often useful to ask what are called *funnelling questions*, such as, 'What happened next?', 'So, then what happened?', and even, 'What was it that you specifically found difficult?' All of these show that you are listening and encourage the other to develop their point.

Another useful technique is to echo what you think is the most important phrase in the form of a question:

> 'I went on the WP course and tried really hard to understand, but I still prefer my typewriter because the WP really worries me.'
> 'You are worried by WPs?'

This is called a *mirroring question* and can be very valuable in encouraging the other to develop their point. However, it is very very important to feed back the *correct* words. If you had responded to the above by using the word 'scared' instead of 'worried', you might have wrongly decoded their message and annoyed them by demonstrating that you were not actively listening and thus caused a breakdown in what might have been building up into an effective communication.

In summary, encouraging questions are:

- *open* – impossible to answer just 'yes' or 'no' to; they begin with 'who', 'what', 'when', etc.

- *funnelling* – such as, 'Can you tell me more about . . .?' or 'What happened then?'

- *mirroring* – using a key phrase to repeat back as a question.

Conversely, limiting questions are:

- *closed* – any question that can be answered by just 'yes' or 'no'

- *leading* – such as, 'Do I need to help? No, of course not'

- *multiple choice* – such as, 'Do you want to go on this course or the next one?'

Staying on target involves not allowing red herrings to creep into the conversation. If you are discussing a topic that is uncomfortable for either of you, there is a risk that red herrings will creep in order to move you away from what it is difficult to discuss. If you are trying to find out why, for example, a subordinate is late for work, they are likely to introduce all sorts of distractions to the point. It is important to acknowledge that you have heard them and then firmly move them back to the point in question. For example, 'I know it is Jane's birthday and I will make a contribution to her present at the end of this meeting, but what I want to focus on is how we can resolve . . .'.

Testing understanding involves summarizing and clarifying what you have heard to check that you are receiving the correct message – 'Am I right in thinking that you have said you are putting me up for the . . . position?' Often when we hear something surprising – good or bad – we assume we cannot possibly have heard correctly, so it is important to check it out. Test your understanding as often as possible. Clarification is useful for checking that you have received the whole message. For example, 'If I could clarify at this point, you are enjoying the job, you like your work but are concerned about the hours you feel are necessary to do it well. How do you think we could resolve this?'

Evaluating the message involves listening with your eyes and with your stomach! Often we get a 'gut' feeling about what we think other people are saying, so check it out. If someone is telling you that they are enjoying their work, but in a flat tone of voice and with withdrawn body language, you might feel that you are not receiving the whole message. You might say, 'I am hearing you say that you are enjoying your work, but I am observing now that you don't seem to be very enthusiastic. I would like to help if there is something we could do to improve it. What might make it more enjoyable for you?'

Neutralizing your own feelings when you are listening is very difficult. The most important thing to remember is that speaking is your turn and listening is their turn. If you are reacting to what they are saying with feelings, you will almost certainly be unable to listen effectively to what they say next. Sometimes, you might have to acknowledge your own feelings out loud before moving back into an active listening mode. For example, when you are receiving criticism, you might need to say something like, 'I am sorry my actions caused you concern, I didn't mean that. Is there anything we can do to resolve the situation?'

Another valuable technique in active listening is the use of silence. We all tend to speak far too much and listen too little. Silence has become something we are uncomfortable with and, therefore, we attempt to fill it up as soon as possible. If we have asked a question or made an encouraging 'hmm' and they have not responded, leave the silence, leave some space. They may be searching for the right way to say something important and if we fill the space, we will never find out what it was. Also, because they will *also* find the silence uncomfortable, they will probably try to fill it and may tell you things that they hadn't intended to but this will give you a truer picture of what is going on.

The final reminder in this section is to clarify, clarify, then clarify again. How do we know that we have received the message they intended to send unless we keep checking back? The following phrases are useful for this purpose:

- 'Am I right in thinking that what you said was . . .?'
- 'If I could clarify, we have agreed that . . .'
- 'I am hearing that . . .'

It may be a surprise to others when we begin to listen more actively, but it is almost always a pleasant surprise and, within a short period of time, you may find that they begin to listen to you more actively, too. Our behaviour has a major impact on how others respond to us, so communicating more effectively with them will encourage them to communicate more effectively with us.

Session 6

•••

Optional elements

Giving and receiving criticism

Discuss why it is so difficult to give and receive criticism. **Ask** the participants what criticism means to them and **list** the responses, which may well include the following:

● being wrong

● being told off

● feeling foolish

● _____

● _____

Suggest that we replace the word 'criticism' with 'constructive feedback' (see further on page 74). **Discuss** the possible definitions of what this could be.

Explain the guidelines to *receiving* feedback positively.

Show these guidelines:

● listen carefully

● clarify exactly what is being said

● assess the feedback

● challenge any non-specifics

● admit any truth about the feedback

● thank the person for giving it

● choose whether or not to change your behaviour as a result.

Discuss these points and ask for questions and comments.

Explain the guidelines for *giving* feedback constructively.

 Show the group these guidelines:

- be clear about what you want to say and why
- check out what the feedback you give says about you, the sender
- start with positives
- link with 'and' rather than 'but'
- refer only to what has been done, not who the person is
- be specific and descriptive
- be selective and communicate as soon after the event as possible
- only refer to behaviour and situations that can be changed
- own the feedback (talk using 'I' statements)
- help them to find alternatives
- be aware that you might be opening a can of worms.

Discuss and ask for questions or comments about these guidelines.

An **exercise**. Set up a role play to practise the above. Ask the participants to each choose a situation (either one coming up soon or one from the past that they now see they could have handled differently) and give them 15 minutes to prepare both their strategy and a brief background scenario for their partners. (If they cannot think of a situation, set an appropriate one, such as giving/receiving criticism for poor time keeping or a poor piece of work.)

Divide the group into threes, each having 15 minutes for role playing their particular situation and receiving feedback. Each has a turn at being the sender, the receiver and the observer. The sender acts in an assertive and constructive way, while the receiver behaves purely as the sender makes them want to respond – not necessarily helpfully. The observer takes specific notes for feedback and keeps time. (See Guidelines for running a workshop, page 146.)

Review what has happened during the exercise in the main group.

Ask participants what they feel they have learned from this session and list useful and interesting points below.

_____

_____

_____

_____

TIME:

BACKGROUND NOTES

When it comes to *giving and receiving criticism*, the vast majority of us have some difficulty and so don't do it very well. And the reason we don't give or receive it very well is that many of us have a difficulty with the concept of criticism. We dislike being wrong, and we want so much to be liked that we want everyone around us to approve of us and what we do, all the time. Another consequence of wanting to be liked is that we don't want to be seen to be finding fault with what someone else has done.

First, to help us reframe the concept, let us dispense with the word 'criticism' and replace it with the term *constructive feedback*. Feedback is an opportunity to review what we do and how we do it with some constructive and objective views from a colleague/superior that will help us grow, develop, and become more effective. This sounds better than criticism already, doesn't it? In order to *receive* feedback constructively, it helps to follow these guidelines:

- listen carefully
- clarify exactly what is being said
- check it out
- challenge any non-specifics
- admit any truth about the feedback
- thank the person for giving it
- choose whether or not to change your behaviour as a result.

Always listen carefully to what is being said. Often when someone makes a criticism about an aspect of our work, we *hear* it as saying that we are a complete failure at the whole thing. So, clarify exactly what it is they are saying – for example, 'Are you telling me that my whole output is unsatisfactory or is there one particular aspect of my work that is below standard?' If it is non-specific, challenge them. For example, if you tell me I am always late, I might say, 'I am aware I was late this morning and once last month, but I am not aware of any other occasions.'

Consider the feedback carefully and, if there is a grain of truth in it, own up immediately. Do *not* justify, just own up. Most of the time, excuses are simply a waste of time. The giver of the feedback may have no interest, at this stage, in the *reason* for your being late – their concern is more likely to be that everyone else was on time and you were late. Later, when you are discussing how to resolve the situation, it may be appropriate for you to say that the British Rail timetable makes it difficult to be on time and you might have to consider other forms of transport.

If the feedback has been given well, in a form that helped you to hear it correctly, and you can see that it might help you, thank the person who has given it to you. It will encourage them to continue to do it well. They may have spent a considerable amount of time and effort planning how to help you, and this always deserves our gratitude. The way to improve how people give you feedback is to thank them when they do it well.

Then, consider whether or not you are going to change your behaviour as a result of the feedback. If you are not, then don't promise that you will never do it again. It is a waste of time and liable to lead to an angry, upset conversation in the near future. If you are, then see how far this person will help you to do so. Try to create an action plan to help you.

Giving feedback constructively also involves following some guidelines. First, it is important to turn criticism into constructive feedback and consider the communication as being part of the process of improving the quality of the work of your department as well as developing the individual. Some guidelines for giving constructive feedback are:

- be clear about what you want to say and why
- check out whether the feedback says more about you than them
- start with positives
- link with 'and' rather than 'but'
- only refer to what has been done, not who the person is
- be specific and descriptive
- be selective and give feedback soon after the event
- only refer to behaviour and situations that can be changed
- own the feedback (using 'I' statements)
- help them find alternatives
- be aware that you might be opening a can of worms.

Before giving feedback, some preparation is crucial. Consider what you want to say and why. If you want to get rid of them from your department and are using a small event as an excuse to criticize them, you will be sending a mixed message. They will be unlikely to be able to satisfy you even if they change their behaviour, so it might be worth considering having a conversation about their future rather than picking on small things that don't really resolve the bigger problem. If you give constructive feedback, will it solve the problem? If so and you are committed to their development and improving the quality of the output of your department, continue with the preparation.

Think about the feedback and whether or not it is possible that it is more *your* concern than theirs. Most of us have issues that we complain about far more than anything else. For example, I have always been concerned about punctuality and am unable to be late for anything. Therefore, I find that punctuality is the issue I complain about most frequently. Sometimes I am aware that I need to relax my standards a little for other people, because mine are so high that very few are likely to be able to live up to them. Check for yourself whether there are some issues that you complain about more than others and whether or not your standards for these issues are realistic.

Whatever feedback you give, it is important to start with positives. When we hear feedback, it tends to sound much worse to us than the sender intends, so start by saying what you are happy with. As we said earlier, any untruth will be obvious, so make sure that you only praise what you feel is truly praiseworthy. For example, make it clear, if it is true, that you like having them in your department and that they are doing particularly well in specific areas.

Avoid making the next word after this praise 'but'. If you tell them they are wonderful 'but . . .', they are likely to ignore all the nice, positive things you have just said. Try replacing 'but' with 'and' – it makes an enormous difference to the way the whole communication is heard; try it for yourself:

> 'I am delighted with the way you have settled into this department and there is one area where I think we could help . . .'.

At this point it may be worth also pointing out that we all tend to receive far more criticism than praise. Given that we all want to be liked and appreciated, perhaps if we praised the behaviour we *do* like, we wouldn't want, or need, to criticize so much because people would be doing more of the things we said we liked. It has been said that one compliment is worth at least ten criticisms and I tend to agree with this.

The next step is to be careful only to give constructive feedback about what the person has done rather than who they are. Telling someone they are hopeless isn't going to be constructive. Telling them that something wasn't done very well and being specific about what it was that wasn't good enough for you *is* constructive. Similarly, telling them that they are *always* late isn't fair because it is almost certainly not the truth. You need to be specific about what it is that you are giving feedback about and when it happened.

Because we are uncomfortable about giving feedback, we tend only to do it when the situation has got out of hand and then tell them *everything* we have been annoyed about during our entire relationship. Some yearly development interviews I have heard of have included up to 12 things that the individual wasn't even aware had been problems! Because everyone finds feedback difficult to listen to, we certainly won't be able to hear more than two or, at the very most, three items, so don't let yourself plan to give more.

Similarly, there should be a statute of limitations on criticism. Telling people that they did something wrong last year is not constructive and is unlikely to help people develop. Give feedback as soon as possible after the event, but only when the individual can cope with it. Think what your reaction would be if it was you. If you have just made a mistake on an important project, it is likely that you will be so upset with yourself that if I, as your manager, call you into my office to discuss it immediately, you will be unable to listen. It would be more constructive (and assertive) to say, 'I appreciate that you are doing all you can to put right the . . . . When you are ready, would you come and debrief with me so that we can take steps to avoid it happening again.'

Only referring to situations or behaviour that can be changed seems obvious, but we all know situations where this has not been the case. For example, telling someone that they are too small to stack the shelves properly in a warehouse isn't very helpful! This may apply to many physical conditions. The yardstick is whether or not the receiver of the feedback believes it can be changed rather than what you believe.

When you actually give the feedback, it is important to speak using 'I' statements. This makes it clear that it is *you* who is concerned about the behaviour, standards, or whatever. If you say, 'Everyone says . . .' this is non-specific and they are likely to find at least one person who doesn't. It also sounds as if you are trying to avoid responsibility for the feedback. Further, it is important not to make it sound as if you have been discussing the problem with everyone else before approaching the individual and that you are not ganging up on the individual. If you say, 'I am speaking on behalf of the management team', it implies that you are all lined up in opposition to the individual. All these things will make it less likely that the individual will be able to properly take in what it is you want to say because they will feel threatened.

Ask the receiver to think about alternative strategies. The more they can come up with their own solutions, the more likely they are to be committed to making a change. If they are unable to do this, offer alternatives and encourage them to make the choice as to what would be best for them.

Plan a follow-up session to review progress and offer your support in the meantime in whatever way is appropriate for them.

Finally, remember that if you are going to give constructive feedback rather than criticism, it is possible that, because you are *communicating* rather than just *talking*, you will hear more than you might want to. For example, if you give feedback about timekeeping and open a discussion about it, you might discover that they don't like working for you and that this is the underlying reason for them being late. Giving feedback can make you realize that unacceptable behaviour is often like an iceberg – only 10 per cent is visible and the other 90 per cent is just as dangerous only hidden. Consider whether you really do want to hear their truth before you start.

Despite all the negative aspects involved, giving constructive feedback is a proven way in which to develop staff and will pay dividends in the long-term effectiveness of all the people who work with and for you.

Saying 'no'

 Ask why it is so difficult to say 'no' and list the reasons, including:

- want be liked
- don't feel we can at work
- _____
- _____

Stress that saying 'no' without feeling guilty or selfish is a personal right. Remind the group of the personal rights reviewed earlier (see page 38) and that even at work they still have this right when they are asked to do things that are not part of their job specification.

List what people have the right to say 'no' to in your organization, such as promotion, overtime, anything against the law/rules of the organization and so on.

_____
_____
_____
_____
_____
_____

Explain that when we want to say 'no' and do so, often it is not heard because people are so unused to being refused a request.

Explain how to say 'no' assertively.

Show the ways in which you can do this (see further page 84):

- decide whether or not you really want to say 'no' and why
- ask for time if necessary
- choose a key phrase that sums up your position and use it
- don't make excuses or lie
- don't allow yourself to be sidetracked
- use empathy for their problem and offer suggestions
- don't take on their problem
- keep repeating your core phrase.

Discuss these actions and ask for questions and comments.

An **exercise:** Either get the group to engage in a role play (such as that outlined in giving and receiving criticism but change the situation to one in which the participant needs to say 'no' – see page 72) or a fishbowl exercise (see page 150). As leader, you may want to take the lead role in the fishbowl exercise and ask volunteers to play out the situation with you. Choose an appropriate situation (such as promotion). Be as manipulative as you like – it is usually the emotional reaction that is most difficult to say 'no' to – but when you want to draw back, because, for example, you are hearing empathy or an assertive 'no' with suggestions, do so and explain why. Whenever the participant runs out of ideas, ask for the rest of the group to coach them or for other volunteers.

As an optional extra element, after a fishbowl exercise, you may want to ask the group to role play their own particular situations.

Review what has happened during the exercise and ask for questions and comments.

Ask the participants what they feel they have learned and list them.

_____

_____

_____

_____

_____

_____

TIME:

BACKGROUND NOTES

Many people, particularly those who tend to respond passively to situations they perceive as threatening, find it difficult to say 'no'. We all want to be liked, so most of us tend to avoid conflict and agree too readily to others' requests, even when we don't want to.

It is worth considering how you feel when someone close to you refuses your request. We often allow others this right more often than we call on it for ourselves. Thus, it may be extremely irritating when you ask someone to do something for you and they refuse. You might become angry in the short term and wonder whether they like or respect you as much as you thought they did. However, in the long term, particularly if they say 'no' assertively and help you by making other suggestions, it is unlikely to damage your relationship. Also, wouldn't you rather they spoke the truth than have them agree but then fulfil it grudgingly only to keep you happy? This is much more likely to damage your relationship than is telling the truth.

At work, it can be even more difficult to say 'no' than it is to do so to friends because, most of the time, we do not feel we have this option. Our jobs are prescribed and we work for a boss who then has the authority to take sanctions, so we feel we might lose our positions.

However, there are many situations where we do have a right to say 'no' at work and we do not always allow ourselves to exercise this right. For example, regarding changes in our job descriptions, overtime, promotions, and so on.

As we said earlier when discussing passive/aggressive behaviour when we do agree to take on something we do not want to do, usually we do it poorly and, in the long term, it is nearly always better not to take it on in the first place. When we agree to do something we don't want to, we nearly always feel angry and upset about it and this can damage our relationships.

Because it is unusual to say 'no' at work, when we do summon up the courage to do it, this message is often not received correctly. The other side then assumes that we have actually agreed to whatever it is and therefore we end up in an even worse situation than if we had agreed to do it in the first place. This is a major cause of communication breakdown at work.

Thus, it is important to learn how to say 'no' assertively so that it *is* heard and understood as 'no'. Let us look at the list of ways in which we can say 'no' assertively again and look at the points in more detail:

- decide whether or not you really want to say 'no' and why
- take time if necessary
- choose a key phrase that sums up your position and use it
- don't make excuses or lie
- don't allow yourself to be sidetracked
- use empathy for their problem and offer suggestions
- don't take on their problem
- keep repeating the message.

Check whether you really want to say 'no' and why. If you would like the promotion, but are concerned that you will fail, it might be more appropriate to say so rather than turn down the promotion without exploring this further.

If you are not sure what to say or do, ask for time to consider the matter. It is extremely assertive to take time out and is much better than making an instant decision that you may regret later. Listen to what they have to say, explain that you would like some time to think about it (depending on the subject matter, this might be a few minutes to a few days). Ask any questions you need to find out as much as you can and agree a time to come back to them about it.

Whatever amount of time you agree to, stick to it. If you agree to let them know about a possible promotion the next morning, and you still haven't made up your mind, go and tell them so rather than try to avoid them! Being decisive is a quality and strength, but so too is making good decisions that you can realize.

If you are clear that you want to say 'no', choose a key phrase that truthfully sums up your position (that you are comfortable with) and be prepared to repeat it. Try not to justify and give reasons at this stage. This is because very often your reasons can be dismantled and found to be not that important. Try also to use the word 'want' rather than 'can't' – nearly always, it isn't true that we cannot: we could if we wanted to. Try not to apologize too much, either:

> 'I am sorry I don't want to work late tonight.'
> 'I enjoy this job and I don't want to be promoted at this stage.'
> 'I appreciate your support but I don't want to move to Sales.'

Then, move on to acknowledging that you have heard and understood their position before making suggestions:

> 'I understand that this report is urgent. I don't want to stay tonight, but I could come in early tomorrow if that would help.'

> 'I can see that you need someone you trust to take over . . . . I don't want promotion just yet, I feel I have more to learn. Is there anyone else who could do it?'

Don't take on their problem – it is not your responsibility. Don't, for example, take the report and find someone else to do it for you, because then you are only taking over their responsibility. Help them in the best way you can by making suggestions and talking through options.

Be prepared to keep repeating your core phrase until they hear it correctly and understand that you are not going to sort out their problem for them.

Whenever you begin to feel guilty about saying 'no', repeat your message again and offer alternative suggestions. This is one particular situation in which it is important to keep the conversation on target. Very often, if a friend wants you to do something and you refuse, they will bring up all sorts of emotive, manipulative red herrings to make you feel guilty. Keep your cool and repeat your core message to avoid being sidetracked into all sorts of blind alleys.

Remember, such a conversation is about them asking you to do something, *not* about whether you like them or not.

Remember, too, that:

- just because someone else wants something doesn't mean that *you* have to fulfil their requirements.
- when someone says 'no' to *you*, it may be annoying but rarely – if they say it with empathy – does it damage your relationship with them.

Influencing skills

Explain that influence has several dictionary definitions, such as the following.

Show them:

- the power of producing an effect, especially unobtrusively
- the effect of power exerted
- the visible operation of an invisible power
- reasonable inducement
- effect produced by individual character.

Discuss these definitions.

Ask participants to list situations where it would be helpful for them to be more influential.

Explain that everything we do and say has an effect. Ask for examples.

Ask where the source of influencing power lies and **list** the answers:

- being the boss
- knowing the right people
- _____
- _____

Link these points with the following list:

- authority
- control of resources
- expertise
- interpersonal skills.

Discuss these.

Explain the continuum of influencing behaviour (see further page 93).

 Show the diagram of this continuum:

Area of freedom for the subordinate
Use of authority by the leader

| Tells | Sells | Consults | Shares | Delegates |

Discuss the diagram.

Explain *push and pull styles* (see further page 94).

 Show the following lists of features of each of these styles to the group:

- *Push style*
  - works best with authority
  - is high risk
  - gets low commitment
  - is win:lose
  - needs enforcement
  - is most effective in the short term

- *Pull style*
  - works without authority
  - is low risk
  - gets high commitment
  - is win:win
  - is self-enforcing
  - is most effective in the long term.

Discuss these two styles.

Explain that neither style is ideal, but, rather, that we need to be comfortable operating with either style so that we can use them appropriately.

Discuss appropriate uses of both push and pull styles.

Explain the importance of win:win to the creation of a successful, long-lasting outcome. Each side needs to ask:

- 'What have I got that they need/want?'
- 'What have they got that I need/want?'

Discuss how the other person has an impact on our influencing skills.

Explain how concentrating on the *issue* rather than personalities and positions will resolve this.

Stress that we have the power to influence and the communication skills to do it effectively, so it is important to consider what we could use it for.

Explain the importance of preparation.

Ask each member of the group to prepare a situation they have in the past wished they had influenced more effectively or one that they expect to face in the future.

Show the group the following list of questions.

- Who do I wish to influence?
- What is the issue?
- What have I got that they want/need?
- What have they got that I want/need?
- What do I think of them?
- How do I usually behave towards them?
- How do they usually behave towards me?
- How important is this meeting for me?
- What would superman/superwoman do now?
- What are my strengths/influencing powers?
- My strategy is . . . .

An optional **exercise**. Ask the group to divide into threes to role play a situation in which to practise using this list, following the guidelines on page 146.

Review what happened with the whole group.

Ask for questions and comments.

Ask for comments about what has been learned and list the contributions.

_____

_____

_____

_____

_____

_____

TIME:

BACKGROUND NOTES

Making a contribution to your organization will usually involve how effectively you influence others as much as what you actually achieve yourself.

One of the main reasons that we do not influence as effectively as we could is that we do not acknowledge and use the personal power we have. It is important to realize that everything you do and everything you say has an effect. Think about a team and how every member of the team plays an important part in it and makes it what it is. When someone leaves, they are very rarely indispensable, but when they are replaced, the team will change fundamentally.

Margaret Ryan, a management lecturer, published some interesting articles and research on the subject of power and influence during the 1980s and concluded that there are four main areas of influential power:

- authority
- control of resources
- expertise
- interpersonal skills.

Authority is perhaps the most widely recognized manifestation of the power to influence. That is, the user can ensure that someone else does something because they have the power to punish or reward, whether or not this is actually voiced in any way.

Control of resources and expertise are not as widely recognized, but they are just as powerful in influential terms. It is not possible to achieve anything without the knowledge or resources necessary to implement it, so the holders of these valuable commodities have an enormous capacity to influence – if they choose to use it.

Interpersonal skills are perhaps the least recognized source of influential power, but, nevertheless, they contain some of the most dynamic options for influencing in all sorts of situations. Nothing is ever achieved unless it can be communicated. It might be said that the purpose of this workshop is to develop the effective communication skills that allow for an increased power to influence, for the benefit of both the individual and the organization.

The effective communicator has a wide power base of influential interpersonal skills because they can:

- communicate ideas and opinions clearly
- build relationships and create networks
- understand others' views and ideas by using good responsive skills (that is, listening)
- access good motivation and development skills to achieve results.

Going back to the original premise that everything we say and do makes a difference, the effective communicator will, by remaining assertive in difficult situations, influence others to remain assertive rather than reactive.

Now that we have established how much influential power each individual has, what are the most effective ways of using it?

In the 1950s new management concepts were developed that moved thinking away from the purely authoritarian (largely based on observation of the leaders of the forces in the Second World War). These can be summed up by an adaptation of Tannebaum and Schmidt's work on leadership and influencing behaviours (first published in *Harvard Business Review* 1958).

Area of freedom for the subordinate				
			Use of authority by the leader	
Tells	Sells	Consults	Shares	Delegates

At the extreme left of the continuum, the leader tells people what to do and they have little freedom. Moving slightly towards the right, the leader decides, but then sells the decision to the subordinates by suggesting what might be in it for them to comply. In the centre, the leader might call a meeting and ask for opinions before making the decision (which might or might not be influenced by what they have said). Towards the right, the leader shares the decision-making process with the group and they make it jointly. At the extreme right of the continuum, the leader delegates the decision by telling the group what the task is and any parameters that exist before leaving them to make the decision as to how to achieve it.

It is interesting to note that at neither edge of the continuum does either side give up their power or freedom completely. No one can make anyone do anything, so even when we are ordered to take a particular course of action, we may still refuse to do so. At the extreme right of the continuum, the leader will still be responsible for the actions of the staff, so still has the power to change the group's decision.

Researchers were interested in this concept and developed it further. They named the behaviour on the left of the continuum *push style* and on the right *pull style* and drew the conclusions mentioned earlier. To remind ourselves:

- *Push style*
  - – works best with authority
  - – is high risk
  - – gets low commitment
  - – is win:lose
  - – needs enforcement
  - – is most effective in the short term

- *Pull style*
  - – works without authority
  - – is low risk
  - – gets high commitment
  - – is win:win
  - – is self-enforcing
  - – is most effective in the long term.

The differences between the two styles can be summed up by observing that involvement of the subordinate gives rise to motivation and commitment to a good result and is, therefore, self-enforcing. We are less likely to refuse if we are involved in the decision making because we feel some 'ownership' and, therefore, it has an element of 'winning', which makes both sides feel good – each has got something that they want. The only disadvantage of the pull style is that it takes time to have an effect, considerably longer than the push style.

Looking at these lists, it is easy to make a judgement as to which is the most effective, but the important point is that *each* of them is highly effective if used in the appropriate situation. For example, if the fire alarm goes off, it is not appropriate to sit around and discuss what action to take, we should all leave the building immediately. Any crisis needs a *push* response to enable effective action to be taken as soon as possible. Similarly, when time is not a major issue, it may be more appropriate to move towards the *pull* style in order to gain all the beneficial commitment and self-enforcement that result.

Anyone who wants to influence effectively needs to develop *all* aspects of the behaviours on the continuum *and* use them appropriately. Each of us will have a natural stance from which we generally operate, but the purpose of this section is to consider its appropriateness and practise the areas that we are not quite so comfortable operating in.

Another aspect of influencing behaviour is how we perform with different individuals. During preparation for a particularly challenging situation where we want to be influential, remembering and answering the following questions is of value.

- Who do I want to influence?
- What is the issue?
- How do I usually behave towards them?
- How do they usually behave towards me?
- How important is this meeting for me?

Often our views of other people are largely formed by what we *think* they think of us, without even checking this out. When we can see that we have decided that they don't think much of us, we write them off and communication is impossible. If you can see that there might be an alternative to their view of you, you can rethink your strategies for how to behave if a successful outcome is important to you. Whether the other person is normally passive or aggressive towards you, the more assertively you manage the communication, the more likely it is that *they* will become assertive again and you have found a way to create an effective communication.

The next stage to consider is creating the win:win possibility. The best way to do this is to consider the question 'What have they got that I want/need?', and then, 'What have I got that they want/need?'

Wherever you decide your greatest sources of influential power lie, it is important to remember that you will need to offer me something that I want or need if you are to influence me. Sometimes you may not know what the other person would value and this might require some research or a conversation with them.

Influencing behaviour is based on concentrating on the issue rather than the position. If it is truly important for you to have an impact on a decision that is to be made, you might be prepared to put your concerns about what you think about the other person on one side. Similarly, if you can state your view powerfully, giving lots of motivation to the other person, you will find that, with practice, you will be able to help them put *their* prejudgements of *you* on one side and they will concentrate on the issue at hand.

Finally, be bold, but responsible. Consider what superman or superwoman would do in this situation. As we have said earlier, most of us have far more power to influence than we think we have or are prepared to use. If you have all this power, consider what you could use it for that would make a positive difference for yourself, those around you and your organization.

If everything we do and say makes a difference, it is well worth considering what the difference is you want to effect. Being aware of your power to influence is the first step. The second is to use it consciously and effectively. Use this list of questions below to help you influence effectively.

- Who do I want to influence?
- What is the issue?
- What have I got that they want/need?
- What have they got that I want/need?
- How do I usually behave towards them?
- How do they usually behave towards me?
- How important is this meeting for me?
- What would superman/superwoman do now?
- What influencing style is most appropriate?
- What power to influence do I have?
- My strategy is _____

  _____

  _____

Delegation

Explain that delegation is part of influencing skills and involves achieving results through other people.

 Ask the group to answer the following questions individually (see further on page 100).

- Is there someone who could do a task better than you?
- Are you really benefiting from the expertise of your staff?
- Is there someone who can achieve an acceptable result even if they do it differently or take slightly longer than you?
- Is there someone who could do the task successfully who is paid less than you?
- Is there someone who could do the task now while you are busy?
- Is there someone who would benefit from doing the task in terms of their development?

 Ask the group why they probably don't delegate enough and

 list their answers, which may include:

- not enough time
- they won't do it properly
- _____
- _____

Ask the group whether everyone wants to be delegated to and what reasons they might have for not wanting it.

Discuss the answers given.

Ask the group to think of benefits of increased delegation.

List the answers given, such as:

● more time to do the things you want to

● better developed staff

● _____

● _____

Explain that a good way of increasing the chances of successful delegation is to communicate the task effectively.

Explain the guidelines for effective delegation (see further on page 102):

● choose the right person

● consult them first

● plan your strategy

● delegate whole tasks

● agree specific outcomes

● take your time

● delegate good and bad tasks

● delegate, then trust the person to complete the task by themselves.

Discuss the guidelines and ask for questions and comments.

Ask the group to consider one task they could delegate on their return to the office and plan it using the following guidelines:

● plan in advance

● clearly state exactly what you want them to do

● explore 'what's in it for them'

- agree methods for assessing performance and time scales
- delegate the authority necessary to complete the task
- ask what support/supervision they need
- stick to what you have agreed and trust them
- agree a review when the task has been completed.

An **exercise**. When the group has completed their preparation, ask them to role play in pairs, each delegating the chosen task to the other in turn.

Review what happened with the whole group.

Ask the group what they have learned from this session and list their answers.

_____

_____

_____

_____

_____

_____

TIME:

BACKGROUND NOTES

Delegation means getting things done through other people (part of the definition of management) and is a valuable part of effective communication. It does not involve abdicating your responsibilities, but rather, empowering and motivating others to achieve results for which you are ultimately responsible.

To start at the beginning of the process, are you delegating enough? Ask yourself these questions.

- Is there someone who could do a task better than me?
- Am I really benefiting from the expertise of my staff?
- Is there someone who can achieve an acceptable result even if they do it differently or take slightly longer than me?
- Is there someone who could do the task successfully who is paid less than me?
- Is there someone who could do the task now while I am busy?
- Is there someone who would benefit from doing the task in terms of their development?

If you answer 'yes' to any of them, you have opportunities to delegate – probably several. Most people have some concerns about the ability of others to do the task as well as or in the same way that we would achieve it and therefore we do not communicate effectively when we delegate. This results in others *not* achieving the task effectively and therefore we reinforce our concerns and continue the pattern of not delegating in the future.

So, why aren't you using your opportunities to delegate? Some commonly used excuses are:

- I like doing the task
- I can do it better myself
- I can't explain what I want
- I don't want to develop subordinates
- I don't want to take the risks involved
- I can't tolerate mistakes
- It takes too long
- I am afraid to.

Understanding your own particular difficulties with delegation will help you move towards resolving them. You might have to consider the benefits to you of trusting your staff to achieve more tasks on their own. The most appropriate person for a task may not be the most qualified. Often, the most qualified is not the most motivated. If you do not delegate, you are likely to suffer professionally. Effective delegation, by its very nature, means allowing for the possibility of failure in a controlled environment. People learn best from experience, and the best experience, still, is to learn from our mistakes.

The person you are attempting to delegate to may have their own barriers to it as well, such as:

- they lack the experience or competence
- they are overloaded with work already
- they are bogged down in trivia
- they want to avoid responsibility.

Being aware that the person you want to delegate to may have such barriers to overcome will help you to listen more actively and develop empathy when you come to delegate.

When you can see the benefits to you of increased delegation, there still comes the difficulty of effectively communicating the task so that you increase the chances of success. First, it is worth considering the following guidelines for effective delegation:

- choose the right person
- consult them first
- plan your strategy
- delegate whole tasks
- agree specific outcomes
- take your time
- delegate both good and bad tasks
- delegate, then trust the person to complete the task by themselves.

Effective delegation requires as much *preparation* as any effective communication. To prepare fully, consider which task you want to delegate and why. Choose the right person to do it. Think about what might be in it for them. Plan your strategy.

When *delegating*, tell them clearly exactly what it is you want them to do. Ask them if they are prepared to take it on. Discuss the benefits for them. Tell them the whole story – the parameters, the time scales, and so on, as well as how the task fits into the bigger picture. As an aside, think about this classic management tale. A man walking past men building with bricks asked them what they were doing. The first said, 'I am cementing one brick on top of another', the second said, 'I am building a wall', and the third said, 'I am building a cathedral'. Guess who was doing the best job?

If they agree to taking on the task, move on to asking them how they intend to achieve it, and agree time scales and methods for assessing progress. Delegate any authority they need to complete the task and ask them what support and/or supervision they require.

Afterwards, *review* what happened, but, meanwhile, apart from agreed support and supervision, you need to trust them to complete the task satisfactorily. If problems occur during the process, ask them how they intend to handle them rather than telling them what they should do. Encourage them to solve their difficulties before giving them your answers. Do not interfere unless they ask you to or unless disaster strikes. At the final review, congratulate them and talk about any lessons learned as well as future development.

The purpose of delegation is to free you to do the tasks that only you can do (and these are what you are really being paid for). Effective delegation will give you more time, make your department more effective, and allow you to consider your next promotion. Side benefits also include a happier department and your having a reputation for developing staff and achieving results.

Delegation is a short-term investment of time that results in a long-term benefit all round.

Role play

Explain that in order to take on new skills and behaviours appropriately, it is important to practise them. When ideas are new, we often feel uncomfortable trying them out and so we avoid implementing them.

Explain that it is important to practise so that the skills become part of our normal behaviour, so that we:

- behave it
- believe it
- be it.

Explain that you are now going to allow each individual to role play an individual situation for which they feel they have gained some new insights into handling through this workshop.

Discuss and resolve any concerns if you can. Restate the agreement on confidentiality, if necessary.

Explain that these role plays will take place in groups of three, to allow the possibility of feedback and support. The session will take approximately $1\frac{1}{4}$ hours: 15 minutes during which each individual prepares their situation and then, in the groups, an hour, during which each person will have 20 minutes (15 minutes to role play their situation and 5 minutes for feedback). Each member of the group will take a turn role playing their particular situation, a turn as receiver, during which they will not necessarily be assertive but will behave as the sender makes them feel, and a turn as the observer.

Ask for questions and comments.

Remind the group of all the things they have learned that have been listed so far, particularly regarding each side of communication (*sending* and *receiving* messages).

Stress that this role play is an opportunity to practise *all* aspects of communication.

Allow the group to prepare for 15 minutes and then move into groups to role play.

Review what has happened in the main group and ask for specific things learned from the role play.

List the contributions made.

_____

_____

_____

_____

_____

_____

TIME:

BACKGROUND NOTES

One of the keys to effective communication is to *prepare*. When we have prepared thoroughly, we are more likely to be assertive and therefore more likely to be able to listen actively. Remember the following:

- the first rule is always prepare
- think ahead
- set clear objectives
- anticipate reactions
- work out your strategy (structure and sequence).

Use the following questions as your preparation check-list.

- Who am I going to communicate with?
- What do I really want to achieve and why?
- Is it SMART (see page 47)?
- Will this resolve the situation?
- What is my fall-back position?
- What do I think their reaction will be?
- What might be in it for them if they agree?
- What could I offer them?
- Am I committed to resolving this amicably?
- How am I going to find out what they want/need?
- What am I going to do if the going gets tough?
- My strategy is . . . .

Use the following as the basis for briefing participants for a role play.

BRIEF FOR ROLE PLAY

Name _____

Playing role of _____

Job title _____

Age and personality _____

Their history _____

_____

_____

_____

Background situation _____

_____

_____

_____

_____

_____

The role play begins with _____

_____

_____

_____

_____

_____

GUIDELINES FOR ROLE PLAYING PERSONAL SITUATIONS

If you want to gain useful practice and feedback in handling a difficult individual or situation, role playing it before enacting it in real life is very helpful.

The first thing to do is to prepare your strategy and consider alternative approaches in case things do not go the way you imagined.

When you are in your group, explain to your partner who you wish them to be, briefly explain what sort of person they are – their age, position, and so on – and the particular situation you want to resolve. Ask them if they have enough information to act on. Do *not* tell them what you are going to tell them, as being able to deal with the other person's reactions is the purpose of the role play and, anyway, in real life they are unlikely to know what you are going to say. Play it as much like real life as possible.

Role play as realistically as you can. If you get stuck, ask for time out and either gather your thoughts before continuing or ask for feedback.

While being given feedback, try to listen as actively as possible. Don't explain why you said or did what you did. Try not to justify it. Instead, listen and see if there is anything you can learn. Remember that it is possible that the real individual concerned will not respond in exactly the same way as your partner has done, but they might (and, from past experience, very often they do).

GUIDELINES FOR PARTNERING A ROLE PLAY

Listen carefully to the brief and ask any questions you feel are important to helping you behave appropriately.

When the role play begins, react instinctively to whatever the 'sender' transmits to you. If you feel irritated, angry, passive, or whatever, then behave like that. The more honestly you can react to them, the more they will learn from the encounter.

Remember that the purpose of the role play is to help the 'sender' practise handling a situation or individual that they find difficult, so the more you can react in the way you feel the subject might the better. If you are too 'nice' and helpful or even difficult or attempt to 'win' the conversation, the 'sender' is less likely to learn very much.

For feedback purposes, it is helpful if you can judge the likely long-term outcome of the conversation. If you have promised to change your behaviour in the conversation, but suspect that in real life you would have been unlikely to be committed to this, say so. Allow the observer to run the feedback, but offer your own comments in addition if you feel you have something to add.

Remember that role plays are not designed to allow you to 'act' but purely to react in a similar way to a described individual or situation to help the 'sender' learn, and bear in mind at all times that you will have your own opportunity to learn in a few minutes.

GUIDELINES FOR OBSERVERS

The role of the observer is not to:

- tell them what they did wrong
- make judgements
- tell them what you would have done.

To help the 'sender' learn from role playing a personal situation, it is important that the observer makes *objective* notes of what they observe. When we are communicating in the real world, we rarely get any objective feedback and this is one way in which a workshop can contribute to the learning.

Observations should point to specific moments at which things change, such as:

> ' I observed that when you said how much you liked having him in your department, he seemed to lean forward and begin to listen actively.'

It is the specific actions, words, or phrases that seem to you to produce an effect that is valuable to the learning process.

The observer can provide powerful feedback for the individual to learn from when this role is fulfilled with care and respect. Also, role plays provide the observer with a scenario from which they may well learn as much for themselves by seeing what works and doesn't work so well in the dynamic communication process, as those enacting it.

Use the following as a check-list to enable you to be as helpful an observer as possible.

- Describe the sender's body language

- Was it congruent with the message?
- Did the receiver appear comfortable?
- Was the objective clear?
- Was a fall-back position revealed?
- Did the sender speak in 'I' statements?
- Was empathy used by the sender?
- How well did the sender listen?
- How well did the sender use questions?
- What was the balance in terms of speaking and listening?
- Was the outcome genuine (that is, do you believe that what they agreed will happen)?
- Note at least three things that specifically helped the communication.

_____

_____

_____

_____

- Note three things that hindered the communication (if any).

_____

_____

_____

Session 7

Summary

Review the main parts of the workshop.

● The differences between talking and communicating.
● What hinders communication.
● Skills to encourage understanding.
● Responsive behaviour.
● Optional elements.

Ask the group for feedback on what they feel are the key lessons they have learned during the course of the workshop. (You may wish to use the lists of things learned made at the end of each of the previous sessions.) It may help if you focus selectively on each key section of the course (you can always note others to return to later).

List the key points made.

Ask the participants to think about what action they will be taking as a result of the workshop.

Review the objectives set at the beginning of the first session and ask them whether they have achieved them.

Remind them that not everything they were doing in the past was wrong. The purpose of this workshop has been to help them in the areas where they did not feel comfortable with the situation or the individual concerned so that they are *even more* effective communicators.

Suggest that, to increase confidence in implementation, it would be useful to consider making small changes in emphasis in the way they communicate rather than throw the baby out with the bathwater. Often a very small percentage change can have a large impact on the outcome.

Stress that an action plan needs to contain a long-term objective (a goal) and then to be made up of small steps to achieve it, like the joke:

'How do you eat an elephant?'
'In bite-sized chunks.'

Explain that a good structure for an action plan consists of:

- a goal (the long-term objective)
- steps to build towards the goal
- support (what or who will help you on your way)
- barriers (what or who might hinder you gaining it and how could you resolve them)
- targets (a SMART action plan made up of steps towards the goal).

Review what SMART objectives are. The letters of the word stand for the following:

- S = simple
- M = measurable
- A = achievable
- R = realistic
- T = timed.

Ask them to prepare an action plan as to how they are going to put into practice what they have learned. Give them a specific amount of time in which to do this.

Prepare a flip chart of the following points, but have it facing away from the participants while they are working.

- Name one thing you particularly liked about this workshop.
- Name one thing you found particularly valuable.
- Name one thing you would like me to consider changing.
- Name one thing you are going to put into action as a result of the workshop.
- How are you going to achieve this action?

When they have finished their action plans, but before you turn the flip chart page to face them, issue a final word of warning.

Stress that making changes to behaviour is often difficult and takes a considerable amount of practise. Remind them of how they learned to ride a bike or swim.

Stress that this programme can only be the first step in taking on new behaviours to encourage effective communication. It is important that they take it slowly when they go back to work. Try out the new skills and modified forms of behaviour in a safe environment rather than taking on the 'sabre-toothed tiger' immediately. Build confidence and practise the skills so that the final goal becomes achievable.

Stress that:

**Failure doesn't happen when you fall down,
only when you don't get up again.**

Explain that this is why support is so important, to pick you up when things aren't perhaps going according to plan, to help you to learn what you can from the difficulty and start again.

Ask for questions and comments before moving on.

Ask each participant in order around the table to answer the points on the flip chart.

Show them the action planning check-list, which will help them act more effectively when they get back to work.

- *Goal* – What do I want to achieve?
- *Activities* – What will I be doing to work towards my goal?
- *Support* – What or who will help me reach my goal? How can I increase my support?
- *Hindering forces* – What or who will hinder me from reaching my goal? How can I reduce these hindering forces?
- *Reality check* – Is it all worth it? If not, review and revise the original goal as necessary.
- *Targets* – Include specific, measurable targets and time scales.

Ask for any further questions or comments and then thank all of them for their contributions and draw the course to a close with an enthusiastic and forward-looking final word – ending on a high note.

_____

_____

_____

_____

_____

TIME:

BACKGROUND NOTES

You have reached the end of the programme and need to move the participants towards a satisfying conclusion. You do this by means of your summary, the purpose of which is to:

- remind the participants of what has been covered
- identify what has been learned
- plan how to put what they have learned into action
- plan how to gain support/review things back at work
- finish on a high note.

To *remind the participants of what has been covered*, it is best to show a list of the main topics of the entire workshop, amending it as necessary, as you go through it, reminding them of the key points you covered in each of the sessions:

- the differences between talking and communicating
- what hinders communication
- skills to encourage understanding
- responsive behaviour
- the optional elements chosen.

To *identify what has been learned*, go back to the notes you made at the end of each section about what they said they had gained. By now they will have learned more from their role plays and you will be able to ask them if now they have the benefit of hindsight, there is anything more that you can add to these notes. The more you can draw from the group, the more likely it is that they will have found the workshop useful and that they will put what they have learned into action. Also, show them again their own objectives for the workshop and ask them if they have been achieved.

The purpose of these two exercises is to complete the session, to remind them of what you and they have been reviewing and what they have learned so that they have all the material necessary to create a plan for how they are going to take this learning away with them and implement it at work.

Making some form of action plan is crucial to encouraging learning to be taken back with them and used in the workplace. It is important to point out that the way to make action plans effective is to make them SMART (see page 114 to remind yourself what the letters stand for).

Saying, 'I am going to empathize more' isn't going to be successful on its own because, although it is very simple, it isn't measurable or timed, so it is unachievable and unrealistic. Saying, 'I am going to practise listening more actively in my meeting with my manager on Monday' is better, but, still, it isn't measurable. What would be even better would be to say, 'I am going to ask Jane to talk to me about her day once a week for 30 minutes so that I can practise listening more actively'.

Writing down what you are going to concentrate on is helpful, but consider how few of our New Year resolutions are ever realized! It is also very easy to lose the piece of paper and the urgencies of work give us an excuse to forget our highly idealized plans and we end up ignoring them. So, as well as writing them down, it is important to speak them, to declare to the other participants at least one thing that we are going to do. Then the group can support them by reminding them when they forget!

Another aspect that is necessary in order to achieve success, but one that is very often overlooked after training sessions, is support. The trainer can help the implementation of action after a course and, therefore, help create tangible, measurable results of the workshop to occur by considering, on the participants' behalves what would support them in their taking their learning back to work and implementing it. The participants' managers might be encouraged to debrief them after the workshop to find out what has been achieved and build a programme of support. They could ask the following kinds of questions:

- What might the participant need to put their plan into action?

- How can the action plan be reviewed?

- How often should this take place?

Alternatively, you might consider arranging a follow-up meeting with the group in, say, three months' time to assess progress and review difficulties or even creating small coaching groups where participants can help each other informally over a period of time.

Without building a support structure to learning and improvement, it is difficult to quantify success and is perhaps one of the reasons why training is not given total commitment by departments within organizations that declare a commitment to training.

To support the participants in implementing what they have learned from this workshop successfully, suggest that they:

- start simple – don't take on the most difficult challenges first, build confidence up with easier successes and work upwards

- don't be put off by failure – debrief with a coach and start again

- learn from success as well as failure. Ask the coach to help you acknowledge successes

- remember the saying mentioned before: Failure doesn't happen when you fall down, only when you don't get up again.

As the leader of the course, you may also find it useful to ask for feed-back for yourself, so that you can learn from the experience, too. Some useful alternative questions to the points that can be written on a sheet of flip chart paper and asked as a closing exercise are the following:

- What did you most enjoy about the workshop?
- What did you find most valuable about the workshop?
- Are there any changes that would be of benefit for future sessions?

Enjoyment often comes from being with colleagues in a different situation and getting to know them better (which all helps communication and team building for the future). I am always amazed how many people say that they found the role plays most valuable even when they have expressed horror at the very idea of doing them originally! Similar comments will help you in the future because you can acknowledge initial concerns and go on to say that the previous workshop found, at the end, that it was the aspect of the programme that they found of most value.

Changes participants think should be considered can involve almost anything, from making the sessions longer or shorter, to holding them away from the workplace, to even dropping the sections they found most difficult. You may not be able to incorporate these changes in the future, but it will give you valuable feedback to consider for the next time, as well as providing an opportunity for the group to give you feed-back and therefore leave them, hopefully, feeling complete.

Remember to finish on a high note. Thank them for their participation, wish them luck, pledge your support (if appropriate), and draw the course to a close on an *enthusiastic* and *forward-looking* final word.

On a personal note, my very best wishes for your workshop – relax and enjoy it as I am sure it will be great! I hope this volume has been of value.

3

....

GUIDELINES FOR WORKSHOP LEADERS

Any workshop designed to improve skills is dependent for its success on a number of factors. These include how well it relates to identified needs, how relevant it is to the real day-to-day work of the participants, how much they are allowed to and do get involved, and more. The previous chapter, running chronologically through the workshop material, was self-contained. Given time to go through this material and making any relevant changes, the workshop that can be run from it can meet many of the criteria for a successful and effective training session. But one other factor is key: that is the way in which the material is conveyed. The effectiveness of training messages, like humour, is dependent on 'the way you tell 'em'.

Naturally enough, this is particularly true of leading a workshop in effective communication skills. The leader will be expected to act as a role model for the subject and, rather than purely *teach* skills, help each participant to find appropriate ways to develop their existing skills. This section is not intended to be a complete run down on training techniques – indeed, your experience may well mean that you do not need this – but, rather, it is designed to highlight key issues, as either an introduction or recap, and provide an overall comment on everything that is necessary to run the sessions described earlier. It is arranged in three sections:

- presentation techniques
- encouraging participation (and how to handle it)
- using exercises such as role plays, which provide valuable assistance in developing effective communication skills

which now follow.

PRESENTATION TECHNIQUES

Presentation

Whoever is leading the workshop, how it will be received is dependent, in part, on the way in which the information is conveyed. So, presentation is very important. But there is more to it than simply putting on a performance that is stimulating and sends people away on a 'high'. Your purpose is to encourage the participants to learn and to change their practices, and thus achieve better results, as a consequence. So, the details regarding how things are done are also important.

This section is designed to highlight key points that can be used to make your presentation more effective. If you can see that your aim is to help people improve their existing skills (in itself an excellent definition of training), then it makes sense to start this review with the group in mind and consider what it is that helps people to learn.

How to ensure that learning takes place

There are several classic ways in which you can positively assist the learning process.

- *Make the message relevant*
  You need to keep the nature of the group in mind throughout the session, to make sure that what you say is in their language, relates to them and their jobs, and fits into their frames of reference. If the group sees that the workshop is tailored to them, representing their situation, and if, above all, they think it will help them do their jobs better or more easily, or both, then they will take an interest and be open to learning. Having clear, stated objectives for the session and seeking the participants' agreement to them is also important for this reason.

- *Order items logically*

  Any message is going to be easier to take on board if it is not a struggle to work it out, so creating a good, clear, and logical path through the content is important. The workshop programme here gives the material a clear structure and the working method has been designed to ensure that this logic is also clear to the participants.

- *Use appropriate emphasis*

  The message must be delivered in such a way that it is easy to concentrate on it. This is helped by a number of factors, such as varying the pace, but also by repetition. Never be afraid to repeat, albeit in a different way, the key elements of the content. By using a combination of methods – presentation of theory, discussion, exercises, and so on – this end can be achieved and the likelihood of participants retaining the essential elements of the material is really enhanced.

With these points in mind, let us now turn to the practical business of how to make the presentation work.

Do not assume that it is easy

Any kind of communication can be, perhaps surprisingly, difficult. In this particular situation, for example, you are faced with the additional confusion of attempting to communicate about how to communicate more effectively! The difficulties can stem from several factors, which, taking a positive view, means you must:

- vary the pace and keep the interest there as people have a natural tendency to let their minds wander rather than concentrate for long periods of time
- work at achieving understanding by avoiding using too much unfamiliar jargon, use visual aids to reinforce points, choose your words carefully and fight people's instinct to make judgements too soon by anticipating – often inaccurately – the whole of the message before it has been completed

- accept that change is always seen as threatening until its usefulness is clear, so if you advocate change, make sure that you explain both how it can be achieved and what good will flow from it (for the participants)

- accept also that there will be plenty of preconceived views and existing memories that act as filters to what you are saying; these may have to be aired and disposed of along the way if a new way is to replace them

- use feedback. The good presenter, and the good group leader, never stops taking in how the group feels (formally, by asking questions, and informally, by observing expressions and reactions) and uses all the information gathered in this way to fine-tune their approach as they go along.

All these points indicate that exercising care and being flexible are necessary.

Preparation

Any difficulties in implementing any of the points mentioned above can be overcome if you follow the three key rules for successful presentation: prepare, prepare and prepare. It is that important. It does not necessarily need to be a lengthy process – certainly, the workshop detailed in this book is deliberately set out in a form that is designed to *minimize* preparation time – but whatever is done must be done thoroughly and systematically. There is no substitute for being truly familiar with the material in front of you, as it will not only facilitate your progress through the material, but will also make you feel more confident and, thus, more able to fine-tune, respond to questions, and digress where appropriate and useful. A key part of preparation is creating guidelines that you can keep in front of you, that act as an effective prompt, and make it easier to work through the content (the workshop material here does just that and allows you to personalize it as necessary).

Positioning the leader within the group

It may seem an obvious thing to say, but the session is not *yours*, it is the *group's*, and all the focus of the preparation and delivery must reflect that. Ask yourself how it will be seen, does it reflect their concerns, can they make use of the learning points, are there any questions you could ask that would enhance their focus on these, and so on. The presenter who prepares only to make it easier for themselves is not generally likely to create a session that will work well for others.

A second point is also important and concerns how the group will see you. Normally, in training, a message is more likely to be taken on board coming from someone the group respects as having expertise in the particular area they are talking about. In a life skill subject, such as communication, though, it is impossible to be an expert – even those of us who have been writing about and training people in the field find ourselves constantly reminded of how much we still have to learn.

Some helpful guidelines for positioning yourself appropriately as the leader of the workshop are to:

- create an atmosphere of mutual respect
- provide a safe environment
- be confident with the material
- be prepared to learn with them.

It will help you enormously if the participants already respect you *before* the session occurs, but your opening remarks can set the tone for the session and gain their agreement to participate fully in the programme (more about this in the next section). It works the other way round too – you need to be prepared to give them *your* full respect. This is often considerably more difficult than it sounds. We all have preconceived ideas about people which hinder us from communicating effectively. As the leader, it is useful to glance round the group before the session starts and check your own feelings. I often find that, within a group of, say, 12 people, there is a member of the group whom I instantly decide is not my sort of person. The only way to clear a path for communication, is to acknowledge the feeling and then put it on one side. All right, they have this and that that I don't like about them, but what else do they have to offer me? If I look at them and listen to them with an open mind, I can usually find something wonderful about them that opens up the possibility of communication.

Any workshop on communicating more effectively is likely to raise situations that the participants personally find difficult and they are unlikely to share their concerns unless you can provide a safe environment. Thus, it is important to raise the issue of confidentiality in your opening remarks. Set some guidelines – which might be that you will not comment on anything they bring up and that it is fine for everyone to discuss afterwards what happened for them as individuals, but that it is not acceptable for them to discuss anyone else or what they might have said during the session. Leave a moment or two for them to think about it and then ask whether anyone would have a problem with this suggestion.

If you are comfortable with the material, which is all part of the preparation process, this will give you the confidence to run a successful session.

So often in organizations, training is seen as an antidote to poor performance. This is apt to produce a group of participants who believe that they are there because they are no good at the subject of the day. It is important to resolve this issue at the beginning of the session. Make it clear that they wouldn't be employed if they were unable to communicate, but that everyone benefits from opportunities to improve in this area. Also say that everyone has situations that they personally find more difficult than others and that this workshop has been designed for them all to learn and practise so that working together becomes even easier and more successful. During the workshop you may find it valuable to share, if you feel brave enough, some of your own difficulties from the past so that the whole group can learn from them.

The purpose of positioning yourself as the leader, therefore, is so that you will be able to help the group to improve their own working lives; you will be acting as a facilitator rather than a teacher. Simply using 'we' rather than 'you' can set the tone for a session that is likely to have a successful outcome.

Struoture

Second only to preparation, in terms of the elements of good presentation, is a sound structure. The workshop material in this book has this built in, but the principles are worth reviewing and are listed now in a way that takes in some of the 'tricks of the trade' for presentation.

One of the oldest maxims for good communication is one that offers excellent advice here: 'Tell them, tell them and then tell them again.' This translates, in this case, into the following guidelines:

- tell them what you are going to tell them (your introduction)
- tell them (the main content), and then
- tell them what you have told them (your summary).

Whatever else you aim to do, these guidelines will help to keep you on track. However, it is not sufficient simply to have a structure – you must make sure that it is visible and develop it as you go through the programme (a process sometimes referred to as 'signposting'). It is hardly possible to indulge in too much signposting as a session proceeds as it is a technique that allows the group to keep everything in context, see how the present topic fits in with what has been covered to date and what will come later, and follow the thread that much more easily than when there is less information of this sort.

So, the overall structure is the classic one of a beginning, a middle, and an end. And each of these have the same structure. Thus, the main segments of the workshop all need their own internal structure. Let's consider these three parts in turn.

The beginning

It is a cliché that 'You only get one chance to make a good first impression', but it is true. It is always right to get off to a good start. People make rapid judgements at the start of the session, thinking, 'Am I going to like this?', 'Is it going to be useful?' A good start gets them in the right frame of mind and is also good for the workshop leader's confidence.

At the beginning of the whole session, all the preliminaries need to be dealt with – the welcome, the administration, and so on – and, at the same time, you must:

- gain the group's attention
- create (or begin to create) the necessary rapport.

The first can be helped by an attention-grabbing opening:

- ask a question (even a rhetorical one)
- use a quotation (to make a point in a memorable manner)
- tell a story, an anecdote, relate a true, recent, or memorable event
- state a striking fact – a statistic, perhaps
- use something visual – a slide, a gesture – to create an impact.

The second is helped by an immediate display of empathy, a focus on the group and how they see things as well as sheer enthusiasm – always potentially infectious – for the event and the topic. The opening is also an opportunity to set the atmosphere for how you want the workshop to be and your role in it.

The middle

This is the core of the session and must:

- present the material in detail
- ensure acceptance of the message
- maintain the attention of the group.

The structure you have worked out and using the technique of signposting referred to earlier (see page 129) will keep the content unfolding logically and smoothly. Using sufficient examples and anecdotes will illustrate what is said, add credibility, and make it live; they will also help maintain interest, especially if the session is also kept reasonably participatory, with questions and discussion acting as the icing on the cake. Make sure that the words you use are sufficiently descriptive, too. For example, you cannot say, 'This is like . . .' too often. As details of the core content come through in this part of the session, the visual aids used will help the participants to maintain their concentration and remember it (they also serve as an extra aid to the leader's memory).

Remember the results of the research carried out for Kodak on how people absorb information, mentioned earlier. Just to recap, the startling results were that 55 per cent of information was reported to be received in a visual form, 37 per cent via the tone of voice used, and only 8 per cent by means of the actual words. Therefore, the more you can use visual displays of the message, the more likely it is to be taken on board.

The workshop material uses a number of primarily check-list-style visuals. The simplest way to show these to the group is to use a flip chart. As most organizations now have overhead projectors (OHP), it is worth also making a short digression here to set out some principles for using these pieces of equipment.

Using flip charts

The greatest advantages of flip charts are that they are easy to use, large enough for the whole group to read, and each sheet can, if required, be removed and pinned or taped to the wall for future reference.

Use the following points as a check-list to ensure that you get the most from flip charts:

- make sure you have enough paper on the stand
- make sure you have pens in different colours and that they will still draw a solid line
- find a position where it is easy for you to write on and easy for the group to read
- make sure you have masking tape or pins to attach finished sheets to the wall
- make sure you write up any lengthy displays in advance
- stand to one side when you have finished writing and face the group
- try not to talk while you are writing (the group won't hear clearly and it is easy to lose the thread of what you are saying or writing)
- write in large, clear, letters whenever possible
- remember that writing on flip charts automatically plays havoc with your spelling, so pay particular attention to this.

Using an OHP

Some care should be taken when using OHPs. They are deceptively simple, but present inherent hazards to the unwary. The following check-list may be of value in helping you to avoid them:

- practise so that you are comfortable operating it and can therefore keep facing the group instead of the screen

- make sure that the flex is out of the way (or taped to the floor)

- check that you have a spare bulb and know how to change it (some machines automatically switch over to a spare, so, in this case, check both of them)

- make sure that it is positioned as you want it – on a stand or table with enough room for notes, and so on – and that it is comfortable for you to use

- stand back and to the side of it – don't obscure the screen

- when using it, check the focus and then turn back to the group

- practise using an acetate roll, running from the back to the front of the machine, on which you can write your own lists (it is much cheaper than using sheets and more flexible)

- only use slides with large enough typefaces or visuals and, when writing on acetate, check that your handwriting is clear and large enough to read

- switch the machine off when you change slides

- if you have a list, practise showing it progressively, using a plain sheet of paper to cover the points you have not got to yet (you will be able to see through it, the group won't)

- remember to stop talking when you put up a new visual as the group will concentrate on the visual and your comment will be missed

- remember to highlight the points you particularly want to emphasize (if you want to keep your slides pristine, put a clear sheet on top for high-lighting on)

- similarly, you can use two slides together to add information (this might include the title of the course or section)

- to point out a particular line or word, use a pen or such, laying it on the slide on the projector (extending pointers are, in my view, almost impossi-ble to use without looking away from the group).

The end

Whether it is the end of the whole session or just a segment of it, the final stage is an important one. There is a need at such points to summarize and to end on a high note. The end is a pulling together of all the points covered – there should be no unanswered questions – and, particularly, participants should leave confident that they have found out something useful and are well placed to implement what they have reviewed.

The very end may consist of some sort of flourish, which could be a quote, a punchy remark, an injunction to act, or, perhaps, a little humour may be appropriate. And the final word will often need to be a 'thank you'. If the group has worked hard, paid attention, and you feel action will follow, then it is not all *your* doing, it is *theirs*, too, and then thanking the participants is certainly in order.

Summary

This is practising what we preach!

The key elements of presentation have been touched on here, but it is a large topic. Essentially, though, nothing is worse than being on your feet, ill prepared and struggling (except, perhaps, being a member of the group experiencing such a workshop!). Preparation, therefore, is the key to getting it right.

By preparing adequately, the workshop will have structure and so the message will be intelligible. Also, the structure then helps you progress smoothly through the whole programme. Such a basis gives confidence to the workshop leader. The rationale behind this book has been to make the process of giving a workshop easier and more certain for you, but the responsibility for the final preparation and implementation lies with you, and attention to detail pays dividends.

Two final thoughts before giving you a check-list that you can use as a summary:

- *timing* stick scrupulously to the timings you work out and, particularly, make sure that participants respect your timings laid down for breaks, exercises, and so on – anything else leads to various degrees of chaos

- any form of workshop (unlike some other sorts of presentation) must be *participatory* and this element has to be accommodated within your smooth progression through the programme.

Check-list of the key principles to remember for effective presentations

Overall

- have clear objectives
- have a sound, stated structure
- focus on the group's point of view
- find the right tone of voice
- expect to *earn* a hearing, not to be given one automatically.

The beginning must respect your audience and make it clear that you will be specifically leading the workshop *for* them and *their* needs. At this point you must:

- get off to a good start
- gain the group's attention
- begin to build a rapport with the group
- make the group want to listen by starting to fulfil their expectations, yet ensure that they keep an open mind about what is to come
- position yourself appropriately (for example, as confident, credible, and so on)

- state your theme, outline your programme (structure) and make it clear that this will suit them (you may want to give them a timetable, but, if you do, stick to the times stated).

The middle is the longest section, and it must:

- maintain and develop interest
- develop the case through a logical sequence of sub-themes
- be illustrated, as necessary, with examples and visual aids
- overcome doubts and concerns, anticipate specific objections and deal with them to ensure that the developing message is seen to be of value to the group.

The end needs to finish on a high note, maybe even a flourish. The concluding part must:

- summarize and pull together all the elements of the message
- stress benefits to the individuals of the group
- make clear that some action is now appropriate
- ask for a commitment
- finish on a memorable note.

Throughout the workshop, the language and gestures (how you appear and the animation you display are just as important as how you sound) used must be:

- clear
- natural
- courteous
- non-judgemental

and put the emphasis on the key points so that the overall impression is of complete professionalism (your goal is for your professional approach to prompt people to think, 'This is the sort of person I could do business with/ learn from').

ENCOURAGING PARTICIPATION

Any training session needs to blend periods of presentation of information *to* the group with periods of participation *by* the group if it is to be truly successful. This is particularly true of a workshop on communication skills. Quite simply, such involvement – taking part in exercises, discussion, and so on – makes it more likely that learning will take place. Even Aristotle is reported to have written that, 'What we have to learn, we learn by doing', and this is backed up by research carried out for IBM and The Post Office. Three groups of people were asked to learn the same process, but were taught how to do it in different ways, and how much they could recall afterwards was measured over a period of time. The results were as follows:

	Told	Told and shown	Told, shown, and experienced
Recall after 3 weeks	70%	72%	85%
Recall after 3 months	10%	32%	65%

It is clear from this that doing the task themselves helped them remember what was involved far better than just being told how to do it or even being told *and* shown how to do it. Prompting involvement can be done using a number of techniques – some as simple as asking a question, others more complicated, such as role playing (more about this on page 146). Let us now review some of the key ways in which you can keep people involved in the sessions.

Involving the participants should start as soon as the workshop begins, so that they realize that they will not be allowed to simply sit and listen, that they will be expected to contribute to the session. If you can introduce some kind of involvement during the opening formalities and introductions, so much the better. Some options for doing this include:

- issuing a simple instruction, such as, 'Would you please fill in the name card in front of you?'

- asking for individuals to speak, perhaps to each other (for example, 'Introduce yourself to your neighbour', or, 'Ask the person next to you what they want to get out of today's session'

- starting a discussion of the brief for the day to get people talking – 'I have run through the objectives, can you think of anything else?'

- the use of a questionnaire to focus each participant on their needs

- the use of a formal 'ice breaker' exercise (see page 20).

Once the session is underway, except for exercises and role plays, much of the participation will involve questions – both handling those asked and using questions yourself to prompt discussion and comment. To avoid questions interfering with the smooth flow of the session, yet to use them to the best effect, involves taking some care with them. The techniques that are best to use vary depending on how questions are being used. We will now consider each type of use in turn.

Managing questions from the group

The first decision you have to make is *when* to take questions. Your decision can be seen as a compromise between different needs because:

- allowing questions at any time can disrupt the smooth flow of the programme, unless you exercise some control

- delaying questions until the end of each segment can frustrate the group and give you a false sense of security that earlier points have been understood and accepted

- discouraging questions, or leaving no time for them, reduces the group's involvement and is poor technique.

You may decide to take questions at each main point. Whatever you decide to do, tell the group the rules and allow enough time in the programme for discussion.

To manage the questions asked, you may find it useful to adopt the following strategy:

- acknowledge the question and the questioner
- ensure that the question has been heard and is understood by the rest of the group
- if you are unsure what the question is getting at, probe to clarify and restate it back to the questioner if necessary
- give short, specific answers where possible and link what you say to other parts of the message of the session when appropriate.

If you opt to answer questions at any time, remember that it is perfectly acceptable to:

- put them on hold for a moment while you finish making the point
- delay answering them (if it fits into, say, the next section, tell them you will return to the point, in which case it is very important to make a note of the question and who asked it in order to remember to cover it later)
- refuse them – some may be irrelevant or likely to lead to too much of a digression – but beware of doing this too often, as it reduces the group's involvement and can be a turn-off, and always explain why you are not allowing a discussion about the particular point in question
- if you don't know the answer to a question, *always* tell the group. Then you can offer to find out or ask if anyone else in the group knows or make a note of it for later (if you attempt to fake an answer, the group will know and you risk losing your credibility) – no one will expect you to know *everything*, so do not worry too much about it, and anyway, if you are well prepared, it is unlikely to happen very often.

Asking questions

Asking questions will help you check that the material has been understood, prompt discussion, and create participation. It also helps to make the group think around a particular point, thus building real understanding of it. People retain information better if they are involved in the finding out process rather than just being told everything.

Questions must be asked *precisely*. There are many examples of questions that encourage people to give misleading answers, such as the journalist's favourite, 'When did you stop cheating on your wife?' What you want to do is to ask questions that give you a genuine answer and we will consider some helpful pointers for achieving this end.

Particularly in a workshop on effective communication, it is crucial to remember that there are no right or wrong answers, as what might be appropriate for one participant may not work for another. Remember when listening to the responses to questions that every answer is potentially right, even if it does not contain the particular point that you were looking for. In this last case you can ask, 'OK, is there anything anyone else would like to add to that?' to see what else emerges.

Most questions are best phrased as *open questions*. These, you will recall from earlier, cannot be answered with a simple 'yes' or 'no' and are therefore more likely to prompt a truthful response that will lead on to a discussion. They typically start with 'what', 'when', 'how', 'where', 'who', and 'why'.

There are also several ways in which you can direct questions:

- *overhead*, that is, putting them to the group generally, which is a useful way in which to open up a subject, such as, 'What do you think would be an appropriate answer here? Anyone?' (if there is no response you can move on to the next method).

- *overhead and then directed*, such as, 'What do you think would be an appropriate answer here? Anyone ? (pause) John, what do you think?', which is useful for getting the whole group to think before looking for an answer from a particular individual

- *direct to an individual*, such as, 'John, what do you think?', which is useful for checking that a particular individual has understood the subject matter

- *rhetorical*, which is one to which you need no response, and this type of question is useful when you want to make a point to one or more people in the group without concentrating on anyone in particular, or to raise a question you would expect to be in the group's mind and then answer it yourself, such as 'What is the point at issue here? Well, perhaps it is . . .'.

All these methods create very controlled discussions – leader, then group member, then leader, then another (or more) group member, but always back to the leader. Two other types will help open up a discussion more and these are:

- *redirected*, which is useful for making others in the group answer an individual's question, such as 'That's a good point, John. What do you think, Mary?'

- *developmental*, which can make the answer to a question a stepping stone for the next point – 'Having established that, James, what do you think about . . .?'

Whichever type of question you use, certain general principles should be applied. For questioning to be effective, the following general method may serve as a useful guide.

- *State the question clearly and concisely* Questions should relate directly to the subject being discussed. Whenever possible, they should require people to think, draw on their past experiences, and relate them to the ideas under discussion.

- *Ask the question first to the group rather than an individual* If the question is directed to an individual first, others are 'let off the hook' and may well not think about the answer. Direct, individual questions are more useful for breaking a general silence in the group or to involve someone who is not actively participating in the discussion.

- *After asking the question, pause* Allow a few moments for the group to consider their answer before you take the next step.

- *Ask a specific individual to answer* The first three steps above start the entire group thinking because they don't know who will be called on to reply. In this way, everyone has to consider each question you ask and be ready to participate. Thus, even those not called on are involved.

To be sure of using an effective questioning method, avoid the following.

- *Asking closed questions* These are questions that can be answered with just a 'yes' or a 'no'. Participants can attempt to guess the answer to this type of question (and might even be correct), but you will not know whether they really understand. 'Do you understand?' is the question *least* likely to give you genuine feedback! Closed questions should not be used if you want the group to use their reasoning power and actively participate in the session.

- *Asking tricky or unanswerable questions* Remember, your purpose is to help people learn and improve, not to antagonize them or make them look small. Difficult questions, yes. Tricky questions, no. Also, keep personalities and sarcasm out of your questions.

- *Asking personal questions* In a workshop such as this, many of the issues raised will prompt personal reactions among the participants. Allow them the space to air them if they wish to, but beware of asking pointed questions. It is usually better to indirectly ask whether anyone has any personal experience of the particular issue that they want to share.

- *Asking leading questions* By leading questions, I mean ones in which the leader indicates the preferred answer in advance, such as, 'Mary, don't you agree that this will solve the problem?' Such questions require little thinking on the part of the participant and, therefore, little is learned. In addition, if Mary didn't agree, she would probably be uncomfortable about saying so, and, thus, you will not receive genuine feedback from her. It is a very confident delegate who will confront the leader and if such a person does this to you, you really are in trouble.

- *Repeating questions* Don't make the mistake of repeating the question for an inattentive member of the group. Doing so simply encourages further inattention and wastes valuable time. Instead, ask someone else to answer. People will soon learn that they have to concentrate.

- *Allowing group answers* Unless written down (and referred to around the group), questions that allow several members of the group to speak are not useful. First, everyone cannot speak at the same time. Second, with group answers you may well find that a few participants try to dominate the session. Third, group answers allow the quiet members of the group not to participate as they should.

The one unbreakable rule all workshop sessions should state, and ensure that it is clearly understood and adhered to, is that *only one person may speak at one time* (and the leader must be the acknowledged referee, deciding who has the floor at any particular moment).

Above all, let your questioning be natural. Ask because you want to know and because you want the information to be shared with the group. Never think of yourself as a question master with a list of questions to be asked, whether they are timely or not. Let your manner convey your interest in the response you're going to get, and be sure your interest is genuine. Forced, artificial enthusiasm will never fool a group.

No matter how effective your questioning technique may become, never consider yourself so clever that you can manipulate the participants. Manipulation is not its purpose. Instead, questioning should be used to promote and build genuine participation and involvement, not to bend the group to your will.

For questioning to be an effective instructional technique, you must create the proper atmosphere in which it can flourish. For example, participants should never fear that they will give the 'wrong' answer because if they do, they will respond only with caution. Remember that in a workshop on effective communication skills, there are no 'right' or 'wrong' answers because communication needs to work for the individuals involved, not adhere rigidly to a set of rules. Also, participants should not be put off from asking questions because they fear they will sound foolish. It cannot be overemphasized that they should be *encouraged* to ask questions, at any time, about anything they do not understand, or to clarify a point to make sure that they have understood it correctly.

USING EXERCISES

Using the question methods outlined in the last few pages may well prompt some lively discussions which can be both enjoyable and profitable for the group as others may be able to throw a new light on a specific issue.

Despite the obvious benefits of such discussions, though, people will still always learn more from actually working at a task. You will remember from the results of the research mentioned on page 137 how important it is not only to *discuss* how to communicate more effectively, but to provide opportunities to *practise* the ideas in a safe environment if the participants are to be able to recall the points made later when they need to use them.

These exercises can take just a few minutes or several hours. For the purposes of the workshop detailed in this book, though, we will limit ourselves to exercises lasting between a few minutes and an hour. These exercises can be conducted in several ways.

- *Individually* There is a place for participants working through an exercise on their own, one benefit being that this allows people to work at their own pace on their own situations or difficulties. However, in a workshop environment, it is better if these are kept short to avoid losing the momentum of the group dynamic.

- *In pairs* Working in pairs gives many of the advantages of individual exercises, yet involves active participation. It is affected by group layout and works best when people are seated so that it is easy for them to turn to their neighbour and go straight into an exercise without moving. (Additionally, an individual exercise can be commented on, or developed, in pairs.)

- *Syndicates* Working in syndicates takes a little longer, and may involve some moving of chairs, but it is valuable. There should not be too many in a syndicate (four to eight is ideal for this subject) and you can make them work best by suggesting that:
  - a chairperson is elected (or nominated) to control discussion and act as timekeeper
  - a 'scribe' is chosen to keep notes of points agreed
  - a 'presenter' is chosen to report back to the whole group.

Whichever forms of exercise you prefer, try to use as many as possible to provide both variety and opportunities for participants to learn in different ways. Also, for the same reasons, whether you allow participants to choose their own partners or you nominate them, try to ensure that everyone works in a small group with every other participant during the course of the workshop.

The ultimate form of exercise – particularly for a workshop on effective communication – is role playing. Role playing needs careful preparation and we now consider how best to do this.

Role playing

Any training that attempts to develop an essentially interactive skill must make a firm link between theory and practice. Role playing is a well proven way to illustrate the material presented *and* give participants opportunities to experience different aspects of communication.

Role playing is a powerful technique, though it is not necessarily the easiest activity to organize if you are to obtain the best results from it. It needs preparation, thought, and care and, ideally, draws on the experience of the workshop leader. That said, its value can be considerable as it provides a safe opportunity to practise with no fear of upsetting real-life relationships or losing business as a result. As such, it may also be regarded as providing an opportunity to experiment in a way that might be regarded as too risky in the real world.

Role playing is not always well conducted. It is important to address any concerns the group may have about it, which, perhaps, are based on prior, and poor, experiences. Acknowledge their concerns and explain that, in real life, we have *no* opportunities to practise our really important communications: it is not possible to ask your manager, colleague, or a client to forget what you have just said so that you can start again! Role playing can never *exactly* mirror real life, but it *does* fulfil the need to practise and get feedback on how you did. Stressing the positive benefits and making it clear that they will be precisely briefed will help overcome any misapprehensions. Ask them whether they are prepared to put their concerns on one side and try to get as much out of it as possible.

If there are one or two in the group who, even after such reassurance, are particularly concerned about role playing, do not panic and decide to delete it from the programme. Acknowledge their concerns and make a note of their names. At the next break explain to them in private that you believe it is important to continue with the planned role plays and then ask them if they are prepared to participate. If not, ask them if they would be willing to act as observers to help the rest of the group get as much as possible from the exercise. Usually, in private, you will be able to discuss their concerns in such a way that they will at least participate as observers if not in the role play itself. If this happens, you will need to choose role plays suited to this arrangement.

Specifically, role playing can provide:

- an opportunity for each individual to obtain constructive feedback on their performance (not least their own perceptions of their performance)
- examples of common occurrences (difficulties, missed opportunities, and so on) for further group discussion
- a prompt to participants to think about, and thus better understand, the other side's situation to create better communication in the future.

Before considering formal role play exercises, it is worth touching on the simplest form of role play, which is fundamentally just an informal enactment of a real-life situation. For example, if you pose a question that leads on to a conversation, such as, 'Imagine that a colleague says . . .', and quote an example of what they might say, then you can ask, 'How would you reply?' If this last question is directed at a chosen participant, with an instruction for them to reply as they would in real life, then a role play-type conversation will occur between yourself and the participant. Such a conversation can be continued for just a moment or for a few minutes, after which the session can return to its formal format. Even though this is not a scheduled role play, it is a role play none the less: people are encouraged to think about the topic, not in intellectual terms, but very much about the practicalities of applying it day-to-day. Yet, there has been none of the fear that can arise when role playing is scheduled, the setting of scenarios, roles and so on.

Before looking more closely at other forms of role play, it is worth setting out some general guidelines. Role playing can fail and, if it does, the cause probably lies among the following:

- overawareness of being observed
- overacting to the observers
- a belief that role playing means acting
- the difficulty of 'performing' in front of one's peers
- poor role play briefing
- incompetent or destructive feedback afterwards
- those not role playing being given nothing to do.

To avoid these things, all role plays should be organized to achieve the following objectives:

- reproduce real life as closely as possible
- provide an opportunity to practise new skills
- develop confidence
- enhance learning by building on success
- experiment with new approaches
- change negative habits and reinforce positive approaches
- fix knowledge and a professional attitude
- promote analytical skills through self-appraisal and observing others.

Also, to encourage constructive feedback, it should be made clear that this does *not* involve:

- telling people what *you* would have done
- giving advice
- telling people what they did wrong.

Constructive feedback builds on the positive aspects of what happened in specific terms, such as saying, 'I observed that when you said his company were regarded as being the market leaders, he leaned forward and seemed to listen more carefully.' When the role play loses its way, don't say, 'You made a mistake' during the feedback part of the exercise, but, rather, comment on what you specifically observed in what was said and done that seemed to you to cause the trouble – say, 'I observed that he stopped listening after you said . . .'. People are usually quick to learn their own general lessons, so the value of an observer is in their providing the participants with the specific points they can learn from.

Forms of role play

- *Role playing in pairs* This is a simple form of role play where one person chooses a situation where they have difficulty in communicating effectively and asks their partner to take the other role. A few minutes are required for the first person to explain to their partner the background to the situation and the personality of the person they are to be. When the situation has been played through, the partner spends some minutes giving feedback on how they felt throughout the conversation and makes specific comments on what it was that made them feel like that. The advantage of this form of role play is that being one of a pair is less intimidating than working in larger groups, but the disadvantage is that there is no objective observation, because the partner also participated.

- *Role playing in groups of three* This is the classic communication workshop role playing format. Using set or personal scenarios, the group take turns in each of the roles. The 'Communicator' is the leading role and this person will be the one trying to achieve effective communication. The 'Receiver' will be asked to respond in whatever manner they feel is appropriate to the personality guidelines they have been given (they are not being asked to communicate effectively – in fact, sometimes it is more helpful if they are particularly difficult). The 'Observer' will take notes throughout the role play regarding any specific points at which they feel the Communicator (not the Receiver) helped or hindered the process. This exercise will last approximately an hour (15 minutes for the role play and 5 minutes feedback for each of the three).

- *Fishbowl role play* This can be enormously valuable, but can also be intimidating early in the session. It is perhaps best kept for when the members of the group have begun to trust each other. It works well when one or more of the group declare a difficulty regarding a particular situation or communicating with a particular individual. Choose one participant and ask them to tell you (and the group) more about the individual or the situation. When they have finished telling you about it, ask their permission to ask for help from the rest of the group to resolve it and then ask them to take your chair in the middle of the group and take on the difficult individual's role. Ask the rest of the group whether any of them have any ideas as to how to resolve the situation and then ask them to role play it. If it goes *well*, allow it to finish and then ask for what they have learned, first the participant with the difficulty and then the rest of the group. If it *doesn't* go well, when either of the role players turn to you, pull out any learning points from it that you can. In either case, you need to ask for any other approaches so that the group maintain their involvement and, hopefully, you can encourage them to think of several different approaches that will help the situation. Remember, there is no one right way to communicate effectively.

- *Empathy role play* This has similar advantages to the fishbowl role play. If one (or any) of the participants has a difficulty regarding a particular situation or individual, it can be very helpful to change roles. When we are given an opportunity to put ourselves in the shoes of the person we are having problems communicating with, we can discover a whole new perspective on the situation. This changing of roles can provide enlightening breakthroughs in understanding that simply cannot be achieved in any other way.

Plenary sessions after role playing

After any of the above forms of role play, it is important to bring the whole group back together to share what has been learned from the role play. This will help maintain the group dynamic and raise ideas that all can learn from. As mentioned earlier, ensure, as much as possible, that individuals share their own experiences and only give positive feedback about other participants, rather than tell 'tales' about others. It is interesting to notice in these sessions how often people realize that they learn just as much from observation as they do from taking the central part.

Using set or personal situations as the scenarios for role playing

Because effective communication is such a personal issue, the participants will learn more if they are prepared to work on their own situations. However, because you may have asked them, at least at first, to try out some completely new ideas, it is often worth using prepared, set situations to avoid clouding the issue with personal prejudices. Then, when it has been agreed that the new ideas are worthwhile, it makes sense to put them into practice for personal situations.

Also, at the beginning of a workshop on effective communication, there may be some concern among the group about declaring what their personal difficulties are. Once the value of role playing using set scenarios has been established, participants show more confidence about sharing personal difficulties.

This may be an appropriate moment to restate how important confidentiality is to the success of this sort of workshop. Before you ask a group to work on personal situations, you may want to remind them of the boundaries of confidentiality that you raised in the opening session. Make it clear, for example, that in any personal role play, it is perfectly acceptable to change names so that they can, if they wish, conceal the identity of the individual they find it impossible to communicate with. Trust in the confidentiality of the group is fundamental to the success of the workshop, and, to encourage leaders, it may be valuable here to point out that, in the hundreds of similar workshops I have been involved with, it is common for the group to have achieved such trust by the second part of the day – so long as the issue has been aired at the beginning.

The use of video

Video recording has become widely used in the development of interpersonal skills and has many advantages, one of the main ones being that participants can observe themselves in action and the need for detailed notetaking is reduced. However, it also has many disadvantages, particularly that it worries many participants and may result in holding them back from real involvement because they fear that they will make a fool of themselves.

My personal opinion is that video is better suited to a more formal skills training session (such as interviewing skills) than this workshop, with its essentially informal format. If, however, in your organization it is commonly used and highly valued, then it may be worth videoing a slightly more formal exercise used in the course of the workshop, such as a fishbowl role play. The following guidelines should be observed when using video:

- check that the equipment is working before the session and that you know how to operate it
- brief the group on why you are using it (for personal feedback on body language and so on and to review specific areas, rather than to assess performance)
- wind the video counter back to zero before starting
- arrange the room so that the camera is able to capture the action without being too intrusive and sit where you can see the counter

- make notes of the number on the tape counter against specific points so that you can make effective use of the video in the review.

The role of the leader of the workshop in any of these exercises is to facilitate. When you have several small groups role playing, you may want to wander between them, checking that things are going well. The objective is to encourage the participants to help each other constructively, but to be available to them when required. Similarly, in the plenary sessions, ask them what they learned before adding other aspects you may have observed.

From the least formal format, mentioned earlier, to the more complicated, role playing is an essential part of this workshop. It should not be underestimated in terms of the care and preparation it requires. If it moves off track, if it goes badly, then people are made to look foolish, which, understandably, they do not like. Providing participants are clear as to the brief and understand the purpose of the exercise, and providing that the leader sets up the situation carefully and makes it a risk-free experience, it cannot help but add to the workshop in a meaningful way.

Its greatest contribution is that it does not test individuals, but creates discussion of examples and situations that the whole group can use, and from which new approaches can be constructed that can be used in the future.

Finally, it should be recognized that not all the people in the group are the same – everyone is an individual, everyone responds to the group situation differently – but you have to work with them all. Ring the changes – in types of exercises and partners – regularly and the chances are high that you will be able to fulfil everyone's requirements.

The use of questionnaires

In order to help participants improve their communication skills and behaviours, it may be helpful to provide clear feedback as to how they are perceived when they communicate. However well intentioned they may be, it is not uncommon for many people to think they come across in one way while objective feedback will produce a completely different picture.

One way in which you can provide objective feedback is to use question-naires. There are many excellent ones available that contain a great range of questions to be answered either by the participant alone and/or by other members of their team. The questions are designed to give a genuine picture of the way in which the individual communicates.

They are designed to be completed before the workshop session and the results annotated so that the participant can see for themselves which side of two-way communication they are more comfortable operating from. It is useful for the workshop leader to receive the results before the workshop starts, so that you can add or minimize emphasis on how to manage the process effectively, as well as the listening and responsive aspects of communication.

The leader must decide whether to display the results of the questionnaires or ask the participants to declare them. On the positive side, it may be useful for the group to see that they all share certain characteristics and that they can all work on these together to improve or even that there is such a broad range of strengths as well as weaknesses in the group that they can all learn from each other. On the negative side, there is a risk that some individuals will feel embarrassed about their results and, therefore, that this will reduce their enthusiasm for the programme right at the very beginning.

In some respects, it does not matter if the results are not openly shared within the group. The important thing is that each individual will know the areas that they might find it valuable to improve and that this will provide a focus for their learning during the course of the programme.

It is certainly worth considering using a questionnaire, but you should inves-tigate several different ones before making a final decision as to which would be of most value. The points to consider are:

- what specifically you want to achieve from it
- how easy it is to fill in and 'score'
- how easy it is in your organization for colleagues to assess each other genuinely
- how much time you have before the session to organize this.

The only way to assess questionnaires is to go through the process yourself. Fill each questionnaire in, 'score' them and assess the results as objectively as you can to see whether or not they are a genuine reflection of your style and whether they concentrate on the specific areas you want to focus on. Ask at least one colleague to fill them in about you and check their results against your own. Also, ask them for feedback on each questionnaire and its 'user-friendly' qualities.

If you do use a questionnaire, the moment in the programme to remind the participants of their scores is when you ask them what their specific objectives for the session are.

The use of training films

However stimulating the training and however much the participants are involved, they may still be stimulated even more by the inclusion of a greater variety of training methodology. A classic way of providing variety in recent years has been the training film. There is a profusion of material available and good ones can do much more than simply provide variety.

First, though, a warning. Some films are promoted as being, or seem to be, self-contained – that is, that their topic can be covered solely by showing a film. This may be true of certain basic issues, but films will nearly always have a more pronounced effect if they are used as an integral part of a longer session. Films and books may have a valuable contribution to make to learning new skills, but, as pointed out earlier, people learn much more effectively when they can experience something as well as being told about it and shown how to do it.

How can films help training become more effective?

- films can provide a different set of memories (by virtue of their visual nature, the characters portrayed, humour, and so on), they put a different complexion on the message, and are a clear aid to retention
- they vary the pace
- they can introduce a topic, particularly when you want to lead in to a discussion
- they can act as a summary at the end of a session

or they can sometimes be used in segments, so that participants watch part of the film, pause for comments or discussion, then return to the film.

However, they are most effective when they play an integral part in the programme, so it is vital to have a clear objective, not only for the course itself, but for the particular section of which the film is to be a part. If you are clear on the points to be made and the result you hope to prompt, then having decided that a film would help, the next step is to select a suitable one. Most providers of training films issue catalogues and it may be worth asking to be included on their mailing lists to help you keep up to date regarding what is available. The main companies also offer a variety of ways of previewing their films and an unbreakable rule should be *never* to use a film you have not seen all the way through and had time to integrate into the session.

There are two main types of film.

- *Right way/wrong way* These may or may not have one continuous story line, but, either way, they tend to start with incidents illustrating how *not* to go about the intended task. Then, in the second part of the film, they not only set out examples of effective practice, but comment on *how* this is done in clear steps. Often these can be suitable for using a section at a time, discussing what has been shown in between.

- *Case studies* These have a strong story line and the training message emerges from the incidents shown. Again, there is usually a clear summary or highlighting of key points. Usually these are best used by showing them without pausing.

Both kinds, and most providers of training films, supply good printed back-up guides for their use. The best of these guides are excellent and may usefully influence your decision as to which film to use.

Films come in a variety of styles. Some are humorous – some to the point where there is a danger that the humour will overwhelm the message – others are based in situations that may or may not be appropriate to your group (a large or small company, say).

In relation to the workshop described in this book, a film or part (it is unlikely that you would want more than one within the content and extent of the material described) may well be useful, but it is by no means essential. If film *is* used, you will obviously need to allow time for it within the programme for the workshop and prepare how you are going to use it. The choice is yours.

One final point: never use a film that does not really suit the session you aim to conduct as it will end up not simply failing to add to the proceedings but actually being a distraction.

From the point of selection onwards, it may make sense to adopt almost a check-list approach to how you use a film. The following points can be used to this end.

- view the chosen film in its entirety
- make notes regarding:
  - significant scenes, points, or dialogue that you may wish to quote or refer to after the film has been shown

- key training points
- additional points (involving 'reading between the lines'), prompts for discussion, specific questions to ask, names of characters, and other details you may want to quote (it is not very professional to be unfamiliar with the material)
- any pause points you want to use when the film is shown to the group (during which you want to enter into a discussion, role play, or use some other method in order to get the message across)

- read and, if useful, annotate the film's 'trainer's booklet' (even when you hire films, these can usually be retained) as these often contain more detail on the topic than appears in the film
- view the film again before using it in the workshop.

ACTION PLANNING

At the end of any training session or workshop, it is vital to encourage the participants to set themselves a personal action plan.

However enlightening you may have been as a leader and however much the participants may have been interested in what was reviewed, it is certain that nothing much will be implemented unless the participant creates some form of plan for moving the learning out of what was merely interesting into action.

As the leader of the workshop, your satisfaction will come mostly from what is actually achieved as a *result* of the session rather than purely from how much you and the participants enjoyed the workshop itself.

Time must be allowed and advice given on how to create an action plan that carries the lessons learned out of the training room and into the real world.

There are several stages involved in putting learning into action. The first is that the participants believe that it will be useful (and, hopefully, the structure of this programme will have ensured that). Second, they believe that it is possible (again, hopefully, through the exercises and role plays, this will have been achieved). Third, they make a commitment to take action (this is provided by a formal action planning session). Fourth, they declare their plans out loud (this is covered in the summary session). Fifth, they allow coaching (that is, that people they have declared their plans to follow up to ask about progress and this is covered in the summary session). You may also want to consider arranging a follow-up session to acknowledge successes and resolve any difficulties.

It is also important that any action plans are SMART (which, you will recall, stands for simple, measurable, achievable, realistic, and timed) to encourage actions to be implemented. The programme gives details and guidelines to follow in this respect.

Action planning will help give you some tangible results over a period of time to measure the effectiveness of your efforts. After all, the only way to encourage your organization to spend resources on training and development is to provide positive results.

Afterword

So, at the end of the workshop (or at the end of reading all the material prior to running the session), what next? It is important to end here by putting certain matters into context.

First, effective communication is a complex social skill. This workshop is designed to allow you to cover all the fundamental techniques that are the basis of being successful in using this skill. Beyond that, success is dependent on practice. This must do two things:

- it must deploy the techniques appropriately – situation by situation, day by day, meeting by meeting – so as to maximize the chances of success in the short term

- it must take place with an awareness of what is being done and how well it is working, to fine-tune its precise application in each meeting to ensure the best chance of success.

Second, it must be accepted that the nature of communication is dynamic, and the inescapable fact is that what works well will change over time and be different for different individuals. All sorts of pressures, competition, attitudes, and so on change over time and affect the outcome. The most effective communicators recognize this and work actively to keep themselves up to date. No one ever learns an infallible way to communicate that can be applied slavishly for ever. In the long term, it can be a lack of fine-tuning that separates the best from the rest, with the less aware lagging behind.

Thus, at the end of the day, it is right for us to refer to what has been covered here as 'fundamental techniques'. There is a saying that a person can have, say, five years' experience or one year's experience multiplied by five. In communication, not only is the former the only way to ensure that your application of techniques is appropriate, it is surely what people want for themselves.

Motivation, so important in the communication process, is surely not enhanced by believing that the process is essentially repetitive.

All this leads us to the following conclusions – and if you are looking for a note on which to end that links what has been done to the future, then perhaps these would be valuable thoughts to leave the group with:

- communication is, and must be, dynamic
- performance can be maintained and improved in the light of this by conscious practice
- the workshop provides the foundations (and should provide some immediate ideas and assistance), but, beyond that, the only coach there is to assist you *all* the time is yourself
- the most effective communicators recognize these things, act accordingly, and achieve better results and greater job satisfaction.

THE FUTURE

After any training session, it is appropriate to look ahead. Whether you are in the training department or you are a line manager responsible for the participants, there are some areas you may want to consider for future coaching and review.

Communication, as has been stressed throughout this book, is a dynamic skill and, therefore, no training programme can be assumed to have resolved any concerns for ever. It is vital to continually review and assess performance and this will involve both the communicator and their manager/coach. Support for the implementation of what has been learned should be included as part of development plans and/or appraisal meetings.

Evidence of commitment is required for change to be ongoing and lasting in any organization and it is worth reviewing how the organization considers and rewards effective communicators. If, for example, senior and respected managers give good, constructive feedback and are seen to be effective communicators, it will be comparatively easy to implement the lessons of this workshop. If, on the other hand, senior managers behave, say, aggressively and are thought to be tough and powerful, it will be very difficult indeed.

Further areas to consider in the development of effective communication skills are the following.

- All areas that involve communication with clients and customers, that is, *marketing, sales and negotiation* skills as well as *customer care* initiatives. Any improvements that can be made in the effectiveness with which your staff communicate with their clients will pay enormous dividends.

- Any areas that involve the employment, management, and development of staff, that is, *introduction to management, interviewing, personnel and appraisal* training. If your staff are more effective in their communication in these areas, you will increase their chances of employing the right staff, developing them to achieve their (and your organization's) potential, and the effectiveness with which they perform the tasks they were employed to do.

This book has concentrated on one-to-one, personal communication skills, but it may well be worth broadening the scope a little and considering developing some of the following areas further, too:

- *presentation skills* more and more managers in organizations are required to communicate formally to a group of people and this raises its own particular difficulties
- *meeting skills* a good deal of work time is spent in meetings and many individuals have difficulties in getting their message across clearly
- *telephone skills* in our modern world where we are linked by telecommunications, the telephone has replaced many of our face-to-face conversations, and, without the usual visual aids that help us understand what we are being told, a rather different set of techniques need to be acquired.

Further reading

This material is designed to be, and is, I hope, self-sufficient, but it is always useful to read around a subject and so I would just like to mention a few books that I have found helpful.

Forsythe, Patrick, *Running an Effective Training Session* (Gower, 1992)
This is a very useful guide to anyone new to training.

There are many interesting and valuable books on effective communication, but I would particularly recommend the following.

Dickson, Anne, *A Woman in Your Own Right* (Quartet, 1986)
Despite being written for women it has wider implications and is a classic work on how to avoid passive/aggressive behaviour in conversation.

Tannen, Deborah, *You Just Don't Understand* (Virago)
Written by an American linguistics professor, this book analyses how men and women speak and what causes some of the major misunderstandings. Fascinating.

Townend, Anni, *Developing Assertiveness* (Routledge, 1991)
A very useful self-development work book for managers.

This book is to be returned on or before
the last date stamped below.
Fine 10c per day

19/09/02

1 2 MAY 2006

30/09/02
P.O.C

21/12/2006

5/5/09

1/11/02
POC

15/11/02
POC

20/05/03

12/5/2006
14/14/05/08